DATE ~~~

SUSTAINABLE THINKING

SUSTAINABLE THINKING

ENSURING YOUR LIBRARY'S FUTURE IN AN UNCERTAIN WORLD

REBEKKAH SMITH ALDRICH

ALA Editions

CHICAGO | 2018

REBEKKAH SMITH ALDRICH (MLS, LEED AP) serves as the coordinator for library sustainability at the Mid-Hudson Library System (New York). Her work has focused on library leadership, governance, marketing, and facility design, all with an eye toward inspiring financial investment in libraries. Rebekkah is the sustainability columnist for *Library Journal*, cochair of the New York Library Association's Sustainability Initiative, and a founding member of the American Library Association's Sustainability Round Table. Named a Library Journal Mover and Shaker, Rebekkah is a frequent national presenter and writer on the topic of leading libraries forward in smart, practical, and effective ways.

© 2018 by the American Library Association

Extensive effort has gone into ensuring the reliability of the information in this book; however, the publisher makes no warranty, express or implied, with respect to the material contained herein.

ISBNs
978-0-8389-1688-9 (paper)
978-0-8389-1696-4 (PDF)
978-0-8389-1695-7 (ePub)
978-0-8389-1697-1 (Kindle)

Library of Congress Cataloging in Publication Control Number: 2017052428

Cover design by Kimberly Thornton. Composition by Alejanra Diaz in the Charis SIL and Proxima Nova typefaces.

♾ This paper meets the requirements of ANSI/NISO Z39.48–1992 (Permanence of Paper).
Printed in the United States of America

22 21 20 19 18   5 4 3 2 1

DEDICATION

This book is for you and those you love.

When you read the acknowledgments, you will be introduced to Jeanne and Jean, two of three women in my life who died of cancer this past year. The third woman who died of cancer this past year was my sister-in-law, Kelly, whom I met in elementary school and who, you guessed it, introduced me to my husband, Adam.

I have debated whether to dedicate this book to them, in their memory. Cancer in humans has many ties to the poor environmental practices of multiple generations. But the more I thought about it, the more I kept coming back to the fact that we all love someone. We all love someone impacted by the disruption caused not only by poor environmental stewardship over many generations but by economic policies that are unfair and by social inequities that lead to discrimination based on ethnicity, sexual orientation, age, and other factors out of our control.

We all love someone who, in the future, will be impacted by environmental, economic, and social policy decisions that are made today. Likely you are driven to do what you do in our profession by this love you have for your family and neighbors. Thankfully, we are powerful and can influence what the future will be.

So, in that vein, this book is dedicated to you, and to those you love, in hopes that tomorrow is brighter than today.

Be well. Be kind. Do good work. Good luck to us all.

CONTENTS

PART III: THE TACTICS

PART IV: RESOURCES

ACKNOWLEDGMENTS

In nature nothing exists alone.

—RACHEL CARSON, *SILENT SPRING*

This book is evidence that no one walks through this world alone.

I am grateful to a *very* long list of colleagues and friends whom I have worked beside and learned from over the past eighteen years.

There is no doubt in my mind that I would never have done half of what I have done professionally without the mentorship, support, and tough love of Joshua Cohen, former executive director of the Mid-Hudson Library System. Josh has helped me create an ethos that has served me well: to do good work and to work on what matters—with a smile. His professional and personal support mean the world to me. Thank you, Josh.

To the member library directors, staff, and trustees of the Mid-Hudson Library System (MHLS) who are always striving to do their best for their communities—thank you. That you invite me to be a part of your story is something I am humbled by. I have learned so much through my eighteen years of working with the sixty-six libraries of MHLS and the directors and thousands of library trustees who step up to make their communities a better place through their public library. We have tried and succeeded, and tried and failed, at many different things. But we've always learned together and together have created some wonderful libraries for the people of the Hudson Valley.

In the past year, we have lost two members of the MHLS family—Jeanne Bogino, former director of the New Lebanon Library, and Jean Ehnebuske, former MHLS trustee and library advocate extraordinaire. I have felt their loss keenly as I wrapped up this book. They were two of my biggest cheerleaders: Jean was the first person to ask for my autograph when I was published in "a real book" in 2012. Jeanne and I started writing our books at the same time (I'm not going to admit how long ago that was!), and we kept each other going when writing got tough (which it always does). They were both earnest, hardworking, caring women who understood the power of public libraries and were willing to fight to make sure others understood the same. I can't help but take this opportunity to acknowledge their influence and reflect on how lucky I was to have them in my life. Jean and Jeanne, thank you for always cheering me on—when doubt sets in I can hear your voices telling me to keep going.

The New York Library Community is a special group of people. Warriors in the fight for library funding, wise and savvy strategists, hardworking and kind, they are the absolute best of what our profession has to offer. Without their strength, vision, and camaraderie, I don't think I would have gotten very far. The New York Library Community would be nothing without the New York Library Association (NYLA) to help us all connect and work together. From my early days on the board of the Leadership and Management Section (LAMS) of NYLA to membership on the NYLA Council to my current roles as the cochair of the NYLA Sustainability Initiative and NYLA Legislative Committee, I have had the distinct pleasure of working with people I admire and whom I aspire to be more like, and with many whom I am proud to call my friends. Thank you for helping to make good things happen. To my longtime LAMS friends—Pat Kaufman, Richard Naylor, Rebecca Lubin, Claudia Depkin, Julie Kelsall-Dempsey, Gillian Thorpe, Frank Rees, Barbara Madonna, and Lauren Comito—thank you. The NYLA Sustainability Initiative (NYLA-SI) might never have happened without your support and encouragement. To the Public Library Section, the Public Library System Directors Organization, Suffolk Cooperative Library System, Suffolk County Library Association, Sandpebble, and Capira—thank you for taking a chance and investing in the NYLA-SI.

To the NYLA Sustainability Initiative Committee members, a heartfelt thank you. Working with you has been a highlight of my career. To work with others who share a vision that libraries can and do and will change the world for the better is energizing and empowering. Your hard work and dedication shine through in all that you do. Thank you for stepping up. I am so excited to see what happens next. We call our committee members co-creators because the answers and work that are necessary to help libraries contribute to creating thriving communities cannot be done alone. We all have to pull together to find our way. I would like to acknowledge the energy, vision, and hard work of my fellow co-creators—you are vanguards!

- Victor Canseco—Sandpebble Builders, Southampton, New York
- Casey Conlin—Haverstraw King's Daughters Public Library, Garnerville, New York
- Jill Davis—Hendrick Hudson Free Library, Montrose, New York
- Claudia Depkin—Haverstraw King's Daughters Public Library, Garnerville, New York
- Kelsey Dorado—New York Library Association, Guilderland, New York
- Deborah Emerson—Wadsworth Library, Geneseo, New York
- Jennifer Ferriss—Saratoga Springs Public Library, Saratoga Springs, New York
- B. Maggie Foster—Mundy Branch, Onondaga County Public Library, Syracuse, New York
- Erica Freudenberger—Southern Adirondack Library System, Saratoga Springs, New York
- Eli Guinnee—Chautauqua-Cattaraugus Library System, Jamestown, New York
- Margo Gustina—Southern Tier Library System, Painted Post, New York
- Geoff Kirkpatrick—Bethlehem Public Library, Bethlehem, New York
- Lisa Kropp—Lindenhurst Memorial Library, Lindenhurst, New York
- Scott Kushner—LaFayette Public Library, LaFayette, New York
- Jill Leinung—Retired, formerly a school librarian for the East Greenbush Central School District, New York
- Stephen Maher—New York University School of Medicine, New York, New York
- Lisa Matte—Jervis Public Library, Rome, New York
- Kate McCaffrey—Northern Onondaga Public Library, Cicero, New York
- Rebecca Miller—*Library Journal* and Floyd Memorial Library, Greenport, New York
- Richard Naylor—Retired, formerly director of the William K. Sanford Town Library, Delmar, New York
- Jessica Philippe—South Central Regional Library Council, Ithaca, New York
- Tameka Pierre-Louis—Queens Borough Public Library, Queens, New York

- Roger Reyes—Suffolk Cooperative Library System, Bellport, New York
- Todd Schlitt—Half Hollow Hills Community Library, Dix Hills, New York
- Jacie Spoon—Cortland Free Library, Cortland, New York
- Judith Wines—RCS Community Library, Ravena, New York

Jeremy Johannessen, executive director of NYLA—you are always "game." #NewYorkRepresent. We do good work together. Thanks for making it fun.

Rebecca Miller, one of the NYLA-SI co-creators, just happens to also be executive editor of *Library Journal.* Her intelligence, articulation, and intense focus on what matters for the future of libraries are part of what makes her so good at what she does. That she rolls up her sleeves and is a participant on the front lines as a library trustee and member of the NYLA-SI is often stunning to me. Goodness knows she could get away with doing a lot less. Her championship of the cause of sustainability in libraries and the opportunities she has given me to more fully articulate my own vision for the future have been life altering. Rebecca, thank you for your support and leadership and for the platform you have given to sustainability in our profession.

When I first met Rebecca, I asked her for a favor—would she please introduce me to Louise Shaper, who was the recently retired director of the Fayetteville (Arkansas) Public Library. She did, and Louise graciously took time to talk to me about her experiences advocating for, building, and operating the first building in Arkansas to be registered for the U.S. Green Building Council's LEED (Leadership in Energy and Environmental Design) certification—her library. Louise's pioneering 2010 article in *Library Journal,* "Let 'Green' Creep," set the stage for the NYLA's and the American Library Association's Resolutions on the Importance of Sustainable Libraries because she talked about the need to embed an "eco-ethic" throughout the library—it wasn't just about the building. That article and subsequent conversations inspired me to think through how you actually do that—how do you *embed* sustainability into the culture of your library? This book is all but an ode to thinking that came out of those conversations. Thank you, Louise—you are grace incarnate.

The friends and connections I have made at the national level over the past seven years have provided me with a wider view of the world. Their interest in and support of the work I have been involved with here in New York have emboldened me to think bigger: members of the ALA Sustainability Round Table, the board of EveryLibrary, my patient-as-a-saint editor Jamie Santoro at ALA Editions, ALA president Jim Neal, ALA Center for the Future of Libraries director Miguel Figueroa, Jessamyn West, Sandra Nelson, Susan Benton, Jeffrey Scherer, Carson Block, Peter Hepburn, Kathy Dempsey, Janie Hermann, Traci Engel Lesneski, Maxine Bleiweis, David Bendekovic, Loida Garcia-Febo—I have found allies in all the right places. Thank you for all you do and continue to do.

For those of you who have a calling, a "life's work," you know that you can't do it alone. The rather long list of people I have thanked here and the hundreds I don't have room to list are proof of that for me. However, there are two other people that I need to acknowledge before I sign off and let you get to reading this book, because without them this book would definitely not exist.

Matthew Bollerman, my cochair of the NYLA Sustainability Initiative, deserves a great deal of thanks and, likely, a lifetime supply of gin for working with me. He is a leader whom I admire and feel lucky to have the chance to work with. As a friend, there can be no one better—the kind who tells it like it is, calls you out when you aren't doing what you should be, and is there when you need him—all with a kind heart. In 2012 he told me to stop just talking about libraries and what they could be doing in the realm of sustainability and to *do something about it.* And then he stepped up to help. Although we have been friends for over a decade, we've definitely tested that friendship in the past few years as we have journeyed together to help libraries embrace the role of sustainability leaders. He is a joy to work with and his intelligence, sense of humor, and good taste in beer have saved the day more than once. Thank you, Matthew—you are one of a kind, and I am thankful to have you in my life.

I devote much of my waking life to libraries: thinking about libraries, working and volunteering for libraries, writing about libraries, researching what libraries are up to . . . I can only do what I do, at the level I choose to do it, thanks to my husband, Adam. He is far more than home IT support and the guy who makes sure there is food in the house. If I had a dollar for every time he tells me "you can do this" when I doubt myself or when he wishes me well on the latest road trip that will keep us apart as I speak in front of library audiences around the country or when I say I need "just" thirty more minutes to write before we can start the movie or when I forget what I'm doing in the kitchen because I'm lost in thought about my work and he still smiles—let's just say that I would be a very wealthy individual. Thank you, Adam, I love you.

INTRODUCTION

My day job is to help libraries get elected.

At the polls, in the state capitol, in the county legislature, and, most important, in the hearts and minds of citizens.

Over the past eighteen years I have worked on more than one hundred library referendum campaigns for operating and capital funds. I have served on my state association's legislative committee for almost a decade. I have worked alongside my colleagues to secure millions of dollars in aid for libraries—locally and at the state level. I am on the front lines of the fight for funding for libraries. And trust me, folks, **it is a fight**.

Library people are, for the most part, **goodness and light**. We believe in common sense. We believe that facts win the day. We believe that democracy works. But we currently live in a world where facts are obscured or ignored, and "alternative facts" are shared by the highest office in the land. We are learning new terms such as *astroturfing* (the practice of masking the sponsors of a message or organization to make it appear as though it originates from and is supported by a grassroots participant). We live in a world in which various political and corporate factions are actively working against what is best for the majority. We live in a world in which money talks.

What does the world look like when democracy can be bought? When free speech is suppressed? When the free press is cast as villainous? What does it look like when a free people can no longer freely govern themselves? What happens to "life, liberty, and the pursuit of happiness" when we are so busy fighting each other over perceived and real slights that we are unable to come together to face some of the biggest crises of our lives?

Much of my job entails listening to influencers—decision makers and opinion leaders—to help create sustainable libraries. Not just the governor, a state senator, or a mayor but everyday taxpayers who are voting whether to invest more of their dollars into their library. What I hear is shifting. What I hear worries me. Increasingly libraries are called *elitist, liberal, nonessential.* Instead of combating that attitude with confidence, library advocates get flustered and defensive, defaulting into a pugilistic stance that only amplifies the opposition's feeling that its proponents are correct.

What our profession needs now is **confidence, determination, and the will to succeed**. Our communities are counting on us.

The heavy lift of advocating for libraries is simultaneously tougher and easier than it has ever been. Tougher because to cut through the noise of modern life and help people understand what we are doing is a massive challenge. Easier because what we do as libraries, and, more important, why we do it, has never been more relevant.

Research I share in this book points to disturbing declines in library use. Library win margins at the polls are shrinking; more libraries are positioned to lose in the coming years. Messaging from libraries is all over the place or nonexistent or, worst of all, untrue.

Do you know that feeling when your sock is falling down inside your shoe as you are walking? It starts out as mildly irritating and then it gets worse. You start to think to yourself, "Ugh. I'm going to have to find a spot to sit down, untie my shoe, and pull up this sock," but you keep walking, hoping it won't get worse. But it does. It gets downright uncomfortable. You might even be limping. That is where I think libraries are right now. It's downright uncomfortable to watch libraries who don't get how they are perceived in the community. It's downright uncomfortable to listen to library leaders who are focused on the wrong things. It's downright uncomfortable to have to go to conferences where heads are in the sand.

It is time to get focused. To sit down, untie the shoe, and pull up the damn sock. Let's do the work so we can stand tall and walk forward with confidence.

That's what this book is about—giving you the foundation and talking points you need to walk into the unknown with confidence that libraries are more important than ever and to never, *never* allow someone to tell you otherwise.

I live libraries. Every day. I love libraries and the people who make them possible. My life's work has been to support those who make libraries **viable, visible, and vital**—to create "sustainable libraries."

People often look at me sideways when I share my title: coordinator for library sustainability. What is that, they ask? Because I am certified as a Leadership in Energy and Environmental Design Accredited Professional (LEED AP), people often assume that my job is isolated to helping build library buildings, and although that is part of my job, it is a smaller part than you might guess. My true job is to ensure that my libraries have the capacity to meet community needs—funding, facilities, leadership, advocacy—these things all work in concert to create a library that is worthy of investment, that matters to those it serves.

Through my unbelievable luck to have had the opportunity to work with some of the best library people in the world—from directors and trustees to library staff and Friends groups to library consultants and architects and, most of all, to the people we serve as librarians—I have learned so much.

I look for patterns. Why did this library succeed? Why do people flock to this library? Why was this program so successful? Why did this vote fail? Why is everything so hard for this library? What makes patrons so loyal to this library?

This book is about those patterns.

This book is about pattern recognition beyond libraries that libraries need to respond to. This book is about the very survival of libraries and our communities.

The world we are living in today has never needed libraries more. Never before has it been so critical that libraries become master tacticians working through a shared strategy that we all need to get behind.

This book is a case for that shared strategy: *sustainable thinking.*

Sustainable thinking, as outlined in this book, helps reset the clock, bringing us back to basics. Our goal is to position the future success of your library in the context of your community's capacity to endure, to bounce back after disruption, and to *thrive*—regardless of what is thrown its way.

In this book, I am asking you to get really good at talking about why we do what we do. I am asking you to live the values that we claim to support throughout all aspects of our operations and outreach.

We need street credibility like never before in order to do the work the world needs us to do. Our commitment to core values such as democracy, diversity, and the public good needs to be reflected in all we do in order for our messaging to resonate.

Now is the time to kick into high gear and use our resources wisely.

To ensure that libraries, and those we serve, are around for the long haul, we must commit to sustainability for our institutions and for our communities.

I believe that libraries are here to **make the world a better place**. That we represent the best of humanity and hope for the future. That our profession is about caring for those who come through our doors, who work in our facilities, and even those who do not directly use library services. We are service professionals, we are information professionals, we are educators—but first and foremost *we are fellow citizens* to those we serve.

Libraries are empowerment engines. We are on the front lines of empowering individuals and communities to make the world a better place. This is a unique and special role we play that we must deliberately embrace. Our power and influence are vast and, in many ways, largely untapped.

We are positioned to effect great change, to make our communities stronger, healthier, safer places to live, work, learn, and play. But we can only do that if people believe in us, and people want to believe in us, they really do.

Thank you for reading this far. I hope you continue. Your library's future may depend on it.

PART I
SITUATION REPORT

DISRUPTION
INSIDE, OUTSIDE, AND ALL AROUND

WELL-MEANT NEWSPAPER HEADLINES LOVE TO QUESTION the vitality and viability of libraries, noting popular opinions that libraries have gone the way of the dinosaur. Reporters and writers across the world, sympathetic to the plight of an institution they view much like their own profession, note the danger of extinction. I've read so many of these articles in the past five years I've lost count.

Dozens upon dozens of newspaper articles, magazine stories, and online news source features follow this same formula: bet you thought libraries were a thing of the past → but wait, there's more to the eye → [insert latest technology or unexpected program] → cute, right? Rarely does a writer miss the opportunity to speak to her own nostalgia about libraries, the printed word, and the quiet solitude of the libraries of her youth. The librarian who changed the writer's life by putting the right book in her hands at the right moment. The fondness that writers and reporters have for libraries is undeniable. The charm, the promise, the hope that libraries have always embodied is still there, everyone!

We are often viewed as passive, awaiting your attention, here to help if you need us. Our bread and butter is storytime and free, high-speed access to the Internet; everything else seems to be cast as the flavor of the month.

Use of libraries, overall, is down. Spin, spin, spin, but the data don't lie. Fewer people are coming through the doors of our libraries. Fewer people borrow items, the same people visit our websites, and we struggle to get people to interact with our electronic resources, save e-books. "That's not the story at my library!" I'll often hear. "People love our library!" "Why, I had fifty kids at this program or the other." That's nice. In fact, that's *great!* I'm so glad to hear it. However, a trend is a trend for a reason—it means that more often than not, use of libraries is down, overall, nationwide.

The Pew Research Center data are invaluable to libraries if you're willing to assess all the data, not just the stuff that makes us look good. The center's 2013 report, *The New Library Patron,* has one of the best headlines about libraries in decades: *"91% of Americans think libraries are important."* Boom! That's amazing, fantastic, and pretty hard to top. However, read a bit farther and you'll see a startling statistic: 30 percent admit—perhaps sheepishly—that they don't quite understand what libraries do anymore.[1] We look different. We're "more than books."

The fact that 30 percent (21 percent of whom earlier answered that they think we are important) are confused about what we do should set off warning bells, like when a hurricane is reclassified to the next highest category. This is our honeymoon period and has been for the past decade. We've tried to tackle it as a messaging issue: okay, we've got a public relations problem—let's fix that; let's learn to talk about ourselves in new ways that will resonate and turn this confusion around.

Valiant efforts are undertaken, regularly, to find new ways to talk about libraries, to find that perfect phrase that's going to turn things around. Yet in 2016, in a new report from Pew, released in April, right at the start of National Library Week thank-you-very-much, came the statistical headline we've all secretly known was coming: "Use of Public Libraries Drifts Down," and no, e-use does not make up the difference.[2] You can read the report for yourself.

Now, you can continue to be in denial (not my library!), talk about how it's not about the numbers (it's all about outcomes!), and, honestly, that's the truth. It should be about the outcomes, about the lives changed, but the numbers are the numbers, and they are used for us and against us in critical moments tied to our funding.

If we are going to be relevant, remain trusted, and be able to truly ride the story line about outcomes to success at the polls and in the hearts and minds of those we serve, we've got a lot of work to do.

A new campaign slogan isn't going to fix this. A new innovative program isn't going to fix this. A cool new application of tech isn't going to fix this. This is big and needs a true, long-haul thinking strategy to address.

The mixed messaging out there about who libraries are and what we do causes confusion among our community members, even our stakeholders. We are many different things to many different people, which means there is a lack of cohesion behind the messaging of why we matter.

Libraries transform. Libraries change lives. Libraries matter. All popular phrases used nationally that say, basically, nothing to someone who isn't a native library user or parent.

We're slipping when we should be shining. There are dozens of beacons out there, libraries "doing it right," who are hardwired into their communities, truly working hand-in-hand with their neighbors to create a better world through library services, but not enough of them. Not enough to stem the tide of uncertainty about the future of libraries. Not enough to turn the tide in Plainfield, Illinois, when an antitax Super PAC turned its sights on the library's building referendum and squashed it. Not enough to quell the inevitable questions we field from family members and friends about the future of libraries.

But we know, we library leaders, we library advocates. We know that libraries *do* matter. We *do* change lives. But we also know that we're often spread too thin, that the impact we're having should be bigger, more obvious. Our institutions, designed for a world that existed decades ago, are struggling in this age of amplified disruption.

We have limped along for a long time, but our honeymoon is over. Outside forces are afoot, directly and indirectly shaping the future of libraries and our communities.

The Americans for Prosperity (AFP) Political Action Committee, a well-known Super PAC underwritten by the Koch brothers, promulgates the Tea Party flavor of the antitax faction: *any tax is a bad tax*. The Koch brothers, two of the richest men on Earth, together worth roughly $43 billion, have sunk funding into AFP that makes this Super PAC a force to be reckoned with. They have helped a fringe movement become mainstream, and in 2016 set their sights on Plainfield, Illinois.

The Plainfield Public Library worked for years to understand what the community needed from it. Through focus groups, surveys, and public town meetings, librarians identified the need for a new library facility.

The library followed a textbook path to build consensus about the new facility and worked hard to present an opportunity to the community that would be affordable and help community members reach their goals for library services in their town.

AFP swooped in after the campaign to pass a referendum to fund the new building got started. The Super PAC funded robocalls to all residents, underwrote signs and ads, and ran a textbook misinformation campaign. The library's $6,000 campaign committee budget could not compete. The referendum was crushed at the polls. The library tried again the next year, lowering the amount requested, but the damage was done. The referendum lost again, by a lot.

Today's civil wars can be won with money if a community is not **cohesive**. A library that is operating with the old handbook is going to limp into the future, its fate uncertain. What is swirling around outside our professional lives is getting weirder and scarier. To weather what is already happening, and what is coming, **we need a loyal base of supporters**—not just users—in our communities that "get" what their library is all about and why that matters in modern society.

The first worksheet of the book, "By the Numbers," can give you a bird's-eye view of how a few people can influence the fate of a community. Voter apathy in local elections and unpredictable voter turnout at the polls can leave a library scrambling to gather enough votes to win. Libraries cut it too close for comfort in more cases than not. Understanding these numbers is critical to being more strategic in the future about who knows about us, who understands us, and who benefits from our services. These are actually three distinct groups, all with the power to sway the financial future of the library.

A new slogan, shiny new tech, and pop-up libraries alone are not going to turn the tide. We need to be strategic, and that's what this book is all about. Being strategic about the future of libraries to the point at which we are sewn so tightly into the fabric of the lives of the communities we serve that it would be unthinkable to underfund, defund, or vote against our libraries.

NOTES

1. Kathryn Zickuhr, Lee Rainie, Kristen Purcell, and Maeve Duggan, "How Americans Value Public Libraries in Their Communities," Pew Internet and American Life Project (December 11, 2013), http://libraries.pewinternet.org/2013/12/11/libraries-in-communities/.

2. "Use of Libraries Drifts Down, While Use of Library Websites Levels Off," Pew Research Center: Internet and Technology (April 6, 2016), www.pewinternet.org/2016/04/07/libraries-and-learning/pi_2016-04-07_learning-and-libraries_0-02/.

BY THE NUMBERS

Hypothetically, if your library went for a vote this year for a building referendum, how many votes would it take to win? _____
(To find the answer, call your board of elections or school district and ask how many people normally come out to vote in the general election or the school budget process in your legally chartered service area.)

How many library cardholders do you have? _____

How many of your library cardholders have actively used your library in the past twelve months? _____

How many donors do you have? _____

How many of your active cardholders and donors are currently registered to vote? _____

Is there a gap between the number of likely supporters of your referendum (users and donors who are registered to vote) and the number of votes you would need to win (50 percent + 1 of the number of voters who come out in a similar election)?

_____

_____

_____

BEYOND OUR WALLS

Is time long, or is it wide?

—LAURIE ANDERSON, ARTIST

IT IS EASY TO HAVE BLINDERS ON. IT IS EASY TO FOCUS on immediate issues of concern, such as the price of e-books, the challenges of managing new staff who are from a different generation than yours, the difficulties associated with being managed by someone from a different generation than yours, or the fact that the air conditioning on the second floor of the library doesn't ever seem to work right. It is hard to keep our eyes on what is going on around us, outside the library, and to synthesize the implications of changes in our world for our library and community.

But that is part of the work: situational awareness.

In the military, officers will ask their soldiers for a "sitrep," a report on the current situation in a particular area. Officers then collate the data from various areas to course correct their plans to ensure that they have the latest intel to base decisions on. To provide a sitrep, soldiers have to be constantly vigilant, and to maintain that vigilance, they cultivate a high level of *situational awareness.*

> Situational awareness is the ability to identify, process and comprehend the critical elements of information about what is happening with regards to the mission. More simply, it's knowing what is going on around you. (Team Coordination Training Student Guide, United States Coast Guard)

Situational awareness today reveals amplified disruption on just about every front—political, economic, technological, environmental, and societal.

I use the phrase *amplified disruption* deliberately. There has always been, and always will be, disruption. However, disruption in the modern world is amplified by a 24/7 news cycle and the content- and engagement-hungry social media landscape. Reaction time is on a fast cycle, causing people to say, do, and think things in ways they did not when they got their serving of the days news from one of three television channels or two newspapers twenty-five years ago.

If a particular area of disruption catches your attention, you can go down the rabbit hole of professional and eyewitness reporting, thousands of people just like you who are sharing their views, vetted and unvetted research about the topic . . . in the quest for information online, the lines quickly blur between fact and opinion. Information literacy? Ha! Best of luck out there.

Political disruption can be felt locally and internationally. Outrageous displays, unexpected characters, obstructionists, placaters, mavericks, coups—all disrupt the work that needs to be done on behalf of ourselves. We suffer through the hackneyed national political sphere—amplified in the age of cable news, niche online publications, Twitter and discussion boards—where various players jockey for position, pander to the camera, searching for the sound bite or the retweetable burn that will launch them into, or keep them in, the spotlight. We watch, internationally, as governments are overthrown, creating chaos and uncertainty, wondering what will happen next?

Economic disruption is happening at a faster and faster pace—from recessions to industry loss, from the antitax movement to disruptive companies and unscrupulous individuals that can change the face of stable markets overnight. Change is happening, and it is happening fast. Our current economy is a delicate thing, leaving larger and larger swaths of people out of the arena of economic security and leveraging others' failure for gain. It is a rapidly moving, twisting, changing "thing" that can make some fabulously wealthy and leave the vast majority fighting for scraps.

Technological disruption is a favorite topic of libraries and the public. Today it is the impact of livecasting your interaction with a police officer, of artificially intelligent video editing that allows anyone to put words in your mouth if you've been videotaped.[1] Tomorrow? Who knows! Tech can disrupt—for better or for worse—in a variety of sectors: the economy, society, politics. Attention to these disruptions is essential for understanding the modern world and participating in it. Basic needs are impacted by technology when governments work to harness the power of tech to deliver services that impact health care, housing, and food. Basic needs are impacted by technology when hackers use programs such as ransomware to hold hostage our personal information or when supposedly secure systems are hacked, releasing sensitive information that can change the landscape overnight. It's not enough for the technological elite to follow changes shaped by tech; it is a topic that impacts us all.

Environmental disruption is perhaps the most brutal and unforgiving disruption of all. It impacts our survivability on this planet. Climate change brought on by decisions made by humans over hundreds of years is now resulting in severe weather patterns that bring on life-threatening floods, droughts, fires, depletion of natural resources, dangerous air that we all breathe. Your mileage may vary on how climate change is impacting your locality, but there is no doubt that food insecurity and access to fresh air, water, and livable places are human issues, not just local issues.

Social disruption is inevitable in the face of the massive disturbances just listed, and this area of disruption exacerbates all others: political, economic, technological, environmental. When people are pitted against each other for access to seemingly limited resources, when others gain from one group's disagreement with another group—we are fractured as a society. As Dr. Martin Luther King Jr. said, "a riot is the language of the unheard."[2]

We are in societal silos, clinging to long-held beliefs, lashing out at one another, disparaging differences of opinion to such a heated degree that violence is breaking out. Are there justified grievances? Absolutely. Is there a civil dialogue that informs change and growth? Not much. When our government is close to nonfunctioning and civic leadership is weakened by the toxicity of the political sphere, the social fabric of our communities becomes frayed and is weakened. Social disruption can take many forms—protest marches, orphaned seniors, racism, terrorism, opioid abuse.

The media influence on our experience today exacerbates challenges. With an endless news cycle to fill 24/7 on cable news and online, various media outlets are growing increasingly desperate to hold on to our attention. They stoop to new lows, amplifying what has always been a profitable tactic: keeping us scared. The media manipulate our worldview to better profit from sensationalizing political disagreements, criminal altercations, and international incidents. This strategy creates a vicious cycle that deepens the divide between segments of our society, decreasing the likelihood that we will work together to address the challenges and opportunities that we are all faced with.

These are "interesting" times we live in with real challenges and real consequences, and it is all happening at once, right now.

This sitrep could make a conscientious professional like yourself feel overwhelmed, helpless, powerless in the face of such chaos. Where to start?

But don't forget: **we're smart**. We have access to all the answers on our shelves, in our databases, and through our neighbors. We can make things better. My hope is that this book will help build your confidence, focus your energy, and encourage you to get to work in a way that makes a lasting impact.

At the beginning of this chapter, I shared a quote from artist, musician, and composer Laurie Anderson: *"Is time long, or is it wide?"* I found this quote in a book by Stewart Brand, best known as editor of *The Whole Earth Catalog,* but this is from his book *The Clock of the Long Now: Time and Responsibility.*

Brand interprets Anderson's question:

> Time can be thought of in terms of everything-happening-now-and-last-week-and-next-week (wide) or as a deep-flowing process in which centuries are minor events (long). The wide view sees events as most influenced by what is happening at the moment. The long view perceives events as most influenced by history: "Much was decided before you were born." The wide view is disparaged as short-term thinking. The long view is praised as responsible.

Librarians are long-haul thinkers. By our very calling we focus on preservation—of access, of information. We focus on lifelong learning, investing time, resources, and energy in educating people of all ages because we believe in their future; we want them to succeed, to go on and do good. We are the epitome of paying it forward. We are consistently thinking about how to persevere in the face of mounting challenges and disruptions. We find a way. No matter what is thrown in our path, we've found a way. So far.

At the end of this chapter you will find a "Disruption Inventory" to help you think through disruption at three different levels: for you personally, for your library, and for your community. Although it is all happening at once to everyone, what we need now is focus. Focus of our energy and resources on repairing and strengthening the social fabric of our communities.

We need to leverage the wide view to improve the long view.

Starting *now,* we need to get our act together and move forward with conviction and purpose. What we do now can lay the foundation for a solid future for libraries if we are working on the right things, sending the right messages, building the right partnerships, and making a difference that matters.

NOTES

1. Jennifer Langston, "Lip-Syncing Obama: New Tools Turn Audio Clips into Realistic Video," *UW News,* July 11, 2017, www.washington.edu/news/2017/07/11/lip-syncing -obama-new-tools-turn-audio-clips-into-realistic-video/.

2. "MLK: A Riot Is the Language of the Unheard," *60 Minutes Overtime,* August 25, 2013, https://www.cbsnews.com/news/mlk-a-riot-is-the-language-of-the-unheard/.

DISRUPTION INVENTORY

What disruptions have already impacted

You personally:
- political
- economic
- technological

- environmental
- societal

_____

_____

_____

_____

Your library:
- political
- economic
- technological

- environmental
- societal

_____

_____

_____

_____

_____

The community your library serves:
- political
- economic
- technological
- environmental
- societal

_____

_____

_____

_____

What future disruptions do you predict will have a negative impact on your community?

_____

_____

_____

_____

What future disruptions do you predict will have a positive impact on your community?

_____

_____

_____

_____

BACK TO BASICS

WHEN OUR LIVES ARE BESIEGED ON ALL FRONTS, IT CAN be disorienting for institutions like libraries to know where to start and how to deploy resources for maximum impact.

Sometimes it is necessary to go back to the basics in order to find our way forward—personally, professionally, and as a citizen.

Abraham Maslow's Hierarchy of Needs is a psychological theory that suggests that people must fulfill basic needs before they can move on to more advanced needs. The hierarchy is represented as a pyramid with the lower levels, the broad base of the pyramid, made up of the most basic needs—the physical requirements for food, water, sleep, and shelter (figure 3.1). Once these lower levels have been attained, people are motivated to seek the higher levels.

Part of my day job is helping my libraries connect with their communities—to listen to residents' hopes and fears about the future and figure out the role their library will play in the coming years. When I conduct focus groups with library nonusers, I also hone in on an assessment of their current perception of libraries as a key factor in helping librarians wake up to the fact that what they think they are selling isn't what the outside world is buying.

After close to 250 focus groups, speaking with more than two thousand people, my unscientific findings indicate that libraries are often seen—by

FIGURE 3.1 ———————————————————————————————

MASLOW'S HIERARCHY OF NEEDS

outsiders and insiders—as assisting with the upper levels of Maslow's pyramid—self-actualization and esteem. However, in times of disruption when changes in society are wreaking havoc or threatening the basic levels of Maslow's pyramid for a person or a community, the upper levels of the pyramid seem very far away. This aspect seems, to me, to be key to why we are always on the defensive, trying to prove we are essential: we do not talk about what we do in the context of the lower half of the pyramid.

There is no denying that people without work, who cannot afford to live in the community of their choice, those struggling to find affordable access to healthy food or clean drinking water, those who place a high value on living in a safe place—these people are going to prioritize little else beyond meeting those basic needs. Those who feel unsafe or out of place in their community are unlikely to participate in meaningful ways to feel a sense of love and belonging among their neighbors.

There is the other end of the spectrum as well: middle- and upper-class families and business owners who feel that any shift in social policy may jeopardize their sense of comfort or safety or result in increased taxes.

This fear leads to a sense of protectionism that in turn leads to a "bunker mentality," creating opposition and entrenchment that can result in divisions in a community.

The residents on both sides of this story often feel that the other is the enemy or that the other doesn't understand where they are coming from. This feeling creates tension, adversarial conversations and campaigns, and a general lack of togetherness.

So, what is a library to do?

A growing number of libraries are reassessing resource deployment to address the basic building blocks of the human condition. From libraries that are embedding social workers on staff to libraries that are working with neighborhood advocates rather than security personnel to address behavior problems in their library to libraries that are stepping up to provide lunch for kids in the summer, I see a shift in attitude toward issues found at the base of Maslow's pyramid from something that must be attended to in addition to library services to a melding of service to all. We can't expect people to get excited about programs about fairy houses and Proust when they are hungry or watching over their shoulder in fear. All things need to happen at once, in a way, and that is impossible for a library to achieve.

A post-Maslow theory adds a sixth layer to the pyramid, above self-actualization: **self-transcendence.** *Self-transcendence* refers to having a higher calling, a higher altruistic goal outside yourself—for your family, neighbors, community, or perhaps the world at large. *That* is where our energy should be focused. Alone we are hopeless, but working together, we are powerful. Appealing to people's desire to be useful, to be helpful, to do meaningful work, to live a better life means we can help support and connect an always growing contingent of people who, like us, want to make the world a better place.

Libraries must embody self-transcendence to appeal to a broad cross section of their community. If we ourselves are conveying a bunker mentality by taking a protectionist stance through our policies and service design, we become less helpful and less appealing. Only through putting our community at the heart of what we do and how we do it can we "transcend" as libraries.

Meeting people where they are in life rather than expecting them to meet you where you are as a library is a key component to a sustainable library.

We must keep in mind that the disruption in today's world strikes at the very foundation of Maslow's Hierarchy of Needs. People's lives and livelihoods are at stake, or people are manipulated to feel that is the case.

Our awareness of and proactive efforts toward minimizing and managing risk in our communities while helping people connect in human ways with one another will serve us well in carrying out our educational mission. An unaware library can quickly lose touch with those it serves and diminish the respect and trust that a library would hope to have in its community. We must be mindful of and present with those whom we serve. An attitude of "we are all in this together" is the only way forward.

Although it can seem too large a challenge to tackle things like access to food, a healthy environment, poverty, community safety, these things will only be stabilized by a *systematic* approach that is coordinated across a community with libraries as part of the strategy.

This chapter's worksheet, "Map the Helpers," provides you the opportunity to map the agencies in your community that are doing good work in specific areas, potential allies with which to find common purpose. No one said we had to tackle these challenges alone.

Many of these challenges are connected and intertwined, making for a tough road to finding solutions, but education is a key component to creating a library, neighborhood, and world that are socially equitable, economically feasible, and environmentally sound. Our work is to best position ourselves to be aware, responsive, and *proactive* as we design the future of our libraries. Library science can be applied to the issues of the day, but only if you are aware of the issues and understand how they are interconnected with the human experience.

MAP THE HELPERS

Create a list of the social services agencies in your community that help residents with the following:

- Emergency preparedness and response
- Housing
- Hunger
- Poverty
- Public health

SURVIVE THE EARTH

IN THE PRECEDING CHAPTER, WE TALKED ABOUT BASIC human needs, essential components to living a happy and healthy life. The most basic things we discussed—food, water, sleep, and, to a large degree, safety—are tied to our natural world.

Our natural world is in rough shape thanks to centuries of reckless consumption of natural resources and profit-driven political decisions that often put earnings and convenience ahead of people and our planet.

We are using natural resources at an unsustainable rate. Access to fresh water is diminishing thanks to pollution and corporate interference.[1] Our oceans are filled with trash; coral reefs are disappearing. Severe weather is becoming more unpredictable and more dramatic. Our food supply is endangered because of soil erosion, a lack of biodiversity, and basic economics. Chemicals in our everyday life make us sick. Wars are fought over oil and soon, some predict, water. These are the building blocks of human life—healthy food, clean water, peace.

The United Nations Intergovernmental Panel on Climate Change (IPCC) report *Climate Change 2014: Impacts, Adaptation, and Vulnerability; Summary for Policymakers* (www.ipcc.ch/pdf/assessment-report/ar5/wg2/ar5_wgII_spm_en.pdf) is significant for many reasons, not the least of which is that it is the first report from the IPCC that changed the narrative from "*saving* the planet" to "***surviving* the planet.**"

Evoking scenes out of dystopian books and disaster movies, the report lays out the harsh reality of what is coming:

- "Until mid-century, projected climate change will impact human health mainly by exacerbating health problems that already exist (*very high confidence*)."
- "Due to sea level rise projected throughout the 21st century and beyond, coastal systems and low-lying areas will increasingly experience adverse impacts such as submergence, coastal flooding, and coastal erosion (*very high confidence*)."
- "Climate change over the 21st century is projected to reduce renewable surface water and groundwater resources significantly in most dry subtropical regions (*robust evidence, high agreement*)."
- "All aspects of food security are potentially affected by climate change, including food access, utilization, and price stability (*high confidence*)."
- "Climate change can indirectly increase risks of violent conflicts in the form of civil war and inter-group violence by amplifying well-documented drivers of these conflicts such as poverty and economic shocks (*medium confidence*)."

As George Carlin so eloquently pointed out in his famous Saving the Planet routine, *"The planet is fine. The PEOPLE are f–ed."*

The planet will survive us, but will we survive the damage we have done to it? The IPCC report clearly states that humans have interfered with the climate and that climate change poses real risks for humans—up to and including death.

These things are happening now. They will continue to happen.

The IPCC report goes on to point out that there are different levels of vulnerability in communities thanks to non-climatic factors and inequalities in our society:

> Uncertainties about future vulnerability, exposure, and responses of interlinked human and natural systems are large (*high confidence*). This motivates exploration of a wide range of socioeconomic futures in assessments of risks. Understanding future vulnerability, exposure, and response capacity of interlinked human and natural systems is

challenging due to the number of interacting social, economic, and cultural factors, which have been incompletely considered to date. These factors include wealth and its distribution across society, demographics, migration, access to technology and information [*Hey! That's us! We are really good at providing access to technology and information!*], employment patterns, the quality of adaptive responses, societal values, governance structures, and institutions to resolve conflicts. (p. 11)

There are only two things we can do: reduce greenhouse gas emissions to lessen the impact of climate change from being worse than is already predicted and, most important, pull together as local and global communities to help each other figure out how to deal with what is coming.

Regardless of our socioeconomic or geopolitical status, the area of disruption with the most potential for widespread suffering and misery is climate change. It is also one of the few things in our world today that could *bring people together* across political ideologies, religions, sexual orientations—we are all human. We all live here on planet Earth. We all love someone who will suffer—in our lifetime or in the future—because of what is going on with the environment.

Use the worksheet titled "My Little Corner of the World" at the end of this chapter to itemize your community's local environmental concerns. Maybe you live in a part of the world concerned about coastal flooding, water or air pollution, lack of easy access to affordable fresh fruits and vegetables. Learn about the world around you, and list those things that threaten your community.

This is an **all-hands-on-deck** moment in history. There is clear urgency and energy around the topics of sustainability and resiliency, and libraries need to be a part of this story because we are a part of this world. It is a common thread, a common cause, and a massive undertaking that will need people like librarians, institutions like libraries, to help lead the way.

If libraries truly live their values, how can they ignore the environmental disruption swirling around us? We all have a responsibility to think through the decisions we are making at every level of our organizations—from operations to outreach and everything in between. Regardless of whether our community has made adaptation in the face of climate change a priority, we need to take ownership and make it a priority. It should be a prerequisite priority, added to the Core Values of Librarianship.

This is crystal clear to me. I've been thinking about it a long time. So I am still patient with my colleagues who respond to my call to action with excuses about attitudes on their board or in their community. "*Climate change* is a trigger phrase." "My community would revolt if I started talking about climate change." "My board would never go for solar panels." Long-held fears that climate change deniers will shame the library and stand in the way of progress are increasingly unfounded. Your board or mayor doesn't like the phrase *climate change*? Fine. Come at it from a different angle.

If you think this topic might be controversial either in your library's governance structure or among climate skeptics in your community—tough. You have a duty as an educator, as a community leader, to find a way to talk about it in a way that results in action. As most leaders have learned the hard way, you've got to "know thy audience."

The truth is, most registered voters (74 percent), regardless of the party they are registered with, say that a range of actors—in government, industry, and civil society—should be doing more to address global warming.[2] The majority of people—whether they vote or not—are concerned or downright alarmed by the impacts of global warming. Research from Yale University and George Mason University has shown that just 9 percent of people are dismissive of global warming.[3]

But Murphy's Law may put one of those rare individuals in an influential position in your library's governance structure or funding path. So **buck up** and get ready to tackle that conversation.

Find common ground. If you take the time to understand where your audience members are coming from and what may fuel their denial that climate change is a major problem, you can find something they do care about: energy security, democracy, economics. Talk about the bottom line: money. It would make more sense to have solar panels on the roof than continue to pay fluctuating energy bills. It would be a smart investment to build a greener library to ensure good indoor air quality that will reduce absenteeism of workers and increase academic performance of users.[4]

Point out that there's really no downside to cleaner air, clean water, food security, and healthier neighbors. At its core, what we are talking about are basic building blocks of human life. There's really no harm in prioritizing humans, and people often feel silly once you frame the discussion from this practical, commonsense perspective.

No one says you have to use the phrase *climate change* to make your point.

Check out the Yale Program on Climate Change Communication (http://climatecommunication.yale.edu/). Climate change communication refers to the "processes by which climate change-related information, knowledge, ideas, emotions, meaning, values, and behaviors flow between individuals and through societies." The program conducts scientific studies on public opinion and behavior to inform decision-making by governments, media, companies, and environmental advocates. The scientists' goal is to help build public and political will for climate action, and they do it well.

We need to get real about what it takes to survive this Earth. We need to be bold and look beyond our own needs as institutions and out into the wider world, leveraging our position in every community to the best advantage for humanity.

No small order.

This sounds like a job for library leaders.

NOTES

1. "Nestlé Faces Backlash Over Collecting Water from Drought-Hit California," *CBS News,* May 9, 2017, https://www.cbsnews.com/news/backlash-bottled-water-nestle/.

2. A. Leiserowitz, E. Maibach, C. Roser-Renouf, S. Rosenthal, and M. Cutler, *Politics and Global Warming, May 2017,* Yale University and George Mason University (New Haven, CT: Yale Program on Climate Change Communication, 2017).

3. "Global Warming's Six Americas," Yale Program on Climate Change Communication (November 1, 2016), http://climatecommunication.yale.edu/about/projects/global-warmings-six-americas/.

4. U.S. Environmental Protection Agency, "Indoor Air Quality in High Performance Schools," https://www.epa.gov/iaq-schools/indoor-air-quality-high-performance-schools.

MY LITTLE CORNER OF THE WORLD

Take a moment to write down the environmental issues facing your neighbors in your part of the world.

_____

_____

_____

_____

_____

_____

_____

_____

_____

_____

_____

_____

_____

_____

THE MOST IMPORTANT THING

IN 2012 I ATTENDED GREENBUILD, THE CONFERENCE OF the U.S. Green Building Council, where I had the distinct pleasure of hearing a presentation by Alex Wilson, founder and past president of the well-respected publication *BuildingGreen* and president of the Resilient Design Institute (RDI). RDI defines resilience as *"the capacity to adapt to changing conditions and to maintain or regain functionality and vitality in the face of stress or disturbance. It is the capacity to bounce back after a disturbance or interruption of some sort."*

I was introduced to *BuildingGreen* when I was pursuing certification as a Sustainable Building Advisor and accreditation as a Leadership in Energy and Environmental Design professional (LEED AP). Mr. Wilson's work first caught my eye because, as a librarian, I was impressed that the publication did not accept advertising, which took away much of the guesswork about whether what I was reading was "greenwashed," a frequent problem in much of the research I did for my coursework.

The other aspect of Mr. Wilson's work that caught my eye was his continued drumbeat for *passive survivability*—an unfortunate term that speaks to a very commonsense approach to constructing facilities: build with an eye toward survivability so that in the aftermath of events such as extended power outages, hurricanes, or terror attacks, our buildings will be able to provide for our basic needs until power, water, or sewer services are restored. This approach made a lot of sense to me.

I was interested in this topic for two reasons. First, I administer the State Aid for Library Construction program in my region of New York State and had two active projects that triggered an awareness of the need for libraries to build more resilient buildings after Hurricane Irene in August 2011. Flooding in the Catskill Mountains, particularly to the degree that we saw because of that hurricane, was something that had never crossed my mind. The devastation, destruction, and despair that we witnessed were things I thought happened in other parts of the world, not in upstate New York. I knew I needed to understand how to build better buildings because we will see more weather like that in my lifetime.

My second reason was a professional secret. I had become rather obsessed with my observation that much of what I was learning about sustainable design for the built environment was translating quite cleanly into my consulting practices to strengthen libraries as organizations. The language of sustainability and resiliency as it was used in the environmental sense was finding its way into my writing and work as a library development consultant. For isn't that what we're all searching for? How to create a library that can withstand the unexpected? Stand tall in the face of uncertainty? Inspire others to support it come what may? I thought I sounded crazy when I talked about it like that. I got a lot of looks that I equated with a pat on the head, the kind of looks that people give you when you've gone a bit over the deep end. I was a little *too* into it. I needed better language to communicate where my thoughts were going.

In a ballroom packed with architects, engineers, construction managers, and others from the building industry, we got a front row seat to a distilled master class on how to build for resilience. Lessons learned from the aftermath of Hurricane Katrina were discussed, and Mr. Wilson shared the ten Resilient Design Principles that RDI developed in light of these lessons learned:

1. *Resilience transcends scales.* Strategies to address resilience apply at scales of individual buildings, communities, and larger regional and ecosystem scales; they also apply at different time scales—from immediate to long-term.

2. *Resilient systems provide for basic human needs.* These include potable water, sanitation, energy, livable conditions (temperature and humidity), lighting, safe air, occupant health, and food; these should be equitably distributed.

3. *Diverse and redundant systems are inherently more resilient.* More diverse communities, ecosystems, economies, and social systems are better able to respond to interruptions or change, making them inherently more resilient. While sometimes in conflict with efficiency and green building priorities, *redundant* systems for such needs as electricity, water, and transportation, improve resilience.

4. *Simple, passive, and flexible systems are more resilient.* Passive or manual-override systems are more resilient than complex solutions that can break down and require ongoing maintenance. Flexible solutions are able to adapt to changing conditions both in the short- and long-term.

5. *Durability strengthens resilience.* Strategies that increase durability enhance resilience. Durability involves not only building practices, but also building design (beautiful buildings will be maintained and last longer), infrastructure, and ecosystems.

6. *Locally available, renewable, or reclaimed resources are more resilient.* Reliance on abundant local resources, such as solar energy, annually replenished groundwater, and local food provides greater resilience than dependence on nonrenewable resources or resources from far away.

7. *Resilience anticipates interruptions and a dynamic future.* Adaptation to a changing climate with higher temperatures, more intense storms, sea level rise, flooding, drought, and wildfire is a growing necessity, while non-climate-related natural disasters, such as earthquakes and solar flares, and anthropogenic actions like terrorism and cyberterrorism, also call for resilient design. Responding to change is an opportunity for a wide range of system improvements.

8. *Find and promote resilience in nature.* Natural systems have evolved to achieve resilience; we can enhance resilience by relying on and applying lessons from nature. Strategies that protect the natural environment enhance resilience for all living systems.

9. *Social equity and community contribute to resilience.* Strong, culturally diverse communities in which people know, respect, and care for each other will fare better during times of stress or disturbance. Social aspects of resilience can be as important as physical responses.

10. *Resilience is not absolute.* Recognize that incremental steps can be taken and that *total resilience* in the face of all situations is not possible. Implement what is feasible in the short term and work to achieve greater resilience in stages. (www.resilientdesign.org/the-resilient-design-principles/)

I was giddy. All ten fit into my draft model of how to create sustainable library institutions (not just facilities) using the language of the environmental sustainability movement.

As part of the program, Mr. Wilson had the audience rank the importance of the ten principles using a mobile app. The result and ensuing conversation are something I will never forget.

The top-ranked principle is one that appears fairly far down the list: number 9.

> *Social equity and community contribute to resilience.* Strong, culturally diverse communities in which people know, respect, and care for each other will fare better during times of stress or disturbance. Social aspects of resilience can be as important as physical responses.

The speaker seemed unsurprised by this turn of events and shared research indicating that communities with a tighter social fabric, those in which neighbors are more connected to one another, have a higher survivability rate in the face of natural and human-made disasters than those that are not.[1]

Let that sink in: in life-threatening situations caused by weather events or humans, communities that are better connected have a higher survivability rate. When you know your neighbors, you have a resource to draw from to find solutions together.

I couldn't stop thinking about what a tremendous role libraries can, should, and do play to increase the resilience of their community. When we work to increase **understanding, respect, and empathy** among the residents of our community, we are helping to potentially save their lives. How huge is that?

The truth is that this is at the heart of what we do as libraries—increase *understanding, respect, and empathy* for others. Through that work, many of life's other challenges can be addressed. Civil discourse, shared problem-solving, and empathy for our neighbors are what this world needs more than just about anything else.

In the aftermath of Superstorm Sandy later that same year, I watched, on the edge of my seat, as libraries in New York responded, not just as sources of information but as boots-on-the-ground support for the neighborhoods that they serve. In many cases librarians were on the ground before the Red Cross arrived. In Queens, librarians were coordinating clothing and food drives, helping people connect with sources for communication, transportation, and other basic needs.[2] Librarians were effective in this setting because of the connections they had established with their neighbors—they were a trusted part of the community's support system on a very basic level.

Our role as a community connector is vital in the sustainability and resilience of a community.

The IPCC report (*Climate Change 2014: Impacts, Adaptation, and Vulnerability*) mentioned in chapter 4 urges *iterative risk management* as a useful framework for decision-making in complex situations, such as the adverse effects of climate change: complex situations are *"characterized by large potential consequences, persistent uncertainties, long timeframes,* **potential for learning,** *and multiple climatic and non-climatic influences changing over time"* (boldface added; www.ipcc.ch/pdf/assessment-report/ar5/wg2/ar5_wgII_spm_en.pdf, p. 9).

The word *iterative* is key. We need to keep learning, keep trying, keep connecting. It is the only thing that will help us in the end, because we don't know what is coming next.

A number of years ago, George Needham, a longtime library consultant and strategist (and now library director), coined the phrase *first restorers* to describe the role of libraries in the face of community crisis. We may not be "siren services" or first responders, putting out a fire or wearing riot gear, but we are a significant part of the solution, helping citizens pick up the pieces and find their way forward.

But we can only be effective as restorers if we've worked continuously to build trust—we can't just show up after a problem has occurred. This mind-set must be continuous: that we are catalysts and conveners who continually work to bring people together.

Libraries are perfectly positioned to assist, if not lead, efforts that speak to managing risk and building resilience as identified in the IPCC report:

- *Local matters.* Adaptations that will strengthen communities are "place- and context-specific, with no single approach for reducing risks appropriate across all settings."
- *Working together.* "Adaptation planning and implementation can be enhanced through complementary actions across levels, from individuals to governments."
- *Recognize and value diversity.* "Recognition of diverse interests, circumstances, social-cultural contexts, and expectations can benefit decision-making processes."
- *Help all be heard.* "Increased capacity, voice, and influence of low-income groups and vulnerable communities and their partnerships with local governments also benefit adaptation."

All four principles match beautifully what libraries are good at already. How fortuitous for us all that *what the world needs most right now is what libraries are already very good at.* How unfortunate that we are not known for playing this role as much as we are known for being book and DVD warehouses.

This chapter's worksheet, "Block Party Planning," asks you to brainstorm a bit about how to help those in your community get to know one another better in hopes that through bringing residents together we can build a stronger community.

The conversation at Greenbuild pointed out to me that we don't know what is coming next, whether it be a hurricane, an act of terrorism, or an economic crisis for either our community or our library. But what we do know, should know, is that the only way to bounce back in the face of these types of events is by working together. The wisdom of the collective is our best bet.

NOTES

1. Barry E. Flanagan, Edward W. Gregory, Elaine J. Hallisey, Janet L. Heitgerd, and Brian Lewis, "A Social Vulnerability Index for Disaster Management," *Journal of Homeland*

Security and Emergency Management 8, no. 1 (2011), https://gis.cdc.gov/grasp/svi/a%20 social%20vulnerability%20index%20for%20disaster%20management.pdf.

2. Ginny Mies, "5 Ways Libraries Support Disaster Relief and Recovery," *TechSoup* (blog), August 25, 2015, http://forums.techsoup.org/cs/community/b/tsblog/archive/ 2015/08/25/5-ways-libraries-support-disaster-relief-and-recovery.aspx.

BLOCK PARTY PLANNING

Brainstorm at least three ways you and your library can help residents of your community feel more like neighbors, people who know, respect, and empathize with each other.

PART II

THE STRATEGY

BEING STRATEGIC

We're here to put a dent in the universe.

—STEVE JOBS, AMERICAN ENTREPRENEUR

DISRUPTION, THOUGH BY DEFINITION UNPREDICTABLE, is a routine part of the library leadership challenge. Libraries are encouraged to be "nimble," "flexible," and "resilient" in a variety of ways—how we budget, how we train staff, how we design our spaces and computer networks. We are expected to be on our toes and ready to pivot at a moment's notice. But what if we extend that risk management mind-set, which is pessimistic, and reframe it to become proactive futurists? What if we align ourselves with the goal of sustainability as a core organizational value? One listed as high as other core values, such as our commitment to free access, a democratic society, literacy, intellectual freedom, and the stewardship of the assets entrusted to us?

If, as we established in the preceding chapter, the most critical aspect of your community's success is a sense of social equity and commonality, have you staked out a strategic position to be recognized as a key agency that contributes to that state?

An activity that I will often do with library trustees who are contemplating a public vote or with a library director who is trying to find a clear path forward is first to ask, *What do you wish the community was saying about the library?* The participants easily can answer this question. Then I ask, *So why isn't your community saying these things today?* This question is usually greeted with a look of consternation, a bit of deflated body language, and the eventual acknowledgment that the library isn't really cohesively portraying an organization worthy of the type of word-of-mouth they wish they were hearing.

Looking in the mirror as an organization and acknowledging that your message is all over the place, that your programs and partnerships don't tell the story of who you want to be, and that sometimes not even your own human resources policies reflect the values you want to be known for is tough. But it's a start.

Libraries are challenged today to tell our story more effectively while deploying services and programs that have a meaningful impact on the communities we serve. This broad leadership challenge requires strategic thinking.

Strategic thinking has been defined as *"deliberately choosing a different set of activities to deliver unique value."*[1] The two words that stand out so prominently in that definition are *deliberately* and *unique.*

- We must make *deliberate choices* to tell the story of who we are and why we are valuable and to position ourselves as a good investment for public and private dollars. True branding of a library requires the layering of your message. It's as the old cliché goes: you can't just talk the talk, you've got to walk the walk. From inside your library (policies, budget decisions, facility operations, human resources policies) to outwardly turned services (collection, technology, programming, partnerships)—all these things add up to tell a story about who you are as an organization. Do they all add up to the message that your library is critical to the sustainability and resiliency of your community?
- We must demonstrate how we are *uniquely positioned* to respond to our local community's hopes, dreams, and aspirations and participate in developing community-based solutions. What can libraries do that almost no other agency can do? We are information professionals. We are trusted organizations. We are community forums. We see the bigger picture. Our strength is in our understanding of how things work, who needs to work together to make things better, and the fact that our library is a platform for others to make good things happen.

*Our buildings, our books, our services, our catalogs must not be
channels of assistance we provide, but part of a powerful
platform that enables our communities to succeed.
This platform is our infrastructure, but it is also the infrastructure
of the community—co-owned.*

—DAVID LANKES[2]

If we believe that our libraries are effective platforms, *empowerment engines*—exactly what the world needs now—then we need to seek a path forward as visible, vital, community-based organizations. That path must ensure the accessibility of library services for generations to come.

Adopting sustainability as a core value of our library, along with other standard core values such as access, democracy, literacy, community, intellectual freedom, stewardship, and adaptability, is a strong strategy to position our libraries for future success. This strategy is not tied to the latest technology, socioeconomic trends, or the evolution of library science; it is a standardized way of thinking that produces a solid foundation from which to respond nimbly to the changes swirling around us *for the long view.*

The most basic definition of sustainability is "the capacity to endure." If we agree that libraries are essential to creating a sustainable community, then our capacity to endure is paramount as well.

This core value needs to be woven into all we do and who we are. From mission statements to long-range plans, from policies to job descriptions, from building operations to outreach activities—we must live that value.

Following this chapter is a worksheet, "Deep Dive: Mission Statement," that asks you to consider the current wording of your library's mission statement through the lens of "sustainable thinking."

The introduction to this book presented the philosophy of Sustainable Thinking. A working definition of sustainable thinking has been created by the Sustainability Initiative of the New York Library Association:

> Sustainable thinking aligns a library's core values and resources with the local and global community's right to endure, to bounce back from disruption, and to thrive by bringing new and energetic life to fruition through choices made in all areas of library operations and outreach. (www.nysl.nysed.gov/libdev/trustees/webinar160908.pdf)

To infuse Sustainable Thinking throughout all we do is a strategy. It is a deliberately chosen set of activities to deliver unique value. Sustainable Thinking requires us to hitch the sustainability of our libraries to the sustainability of our communities. We exist to serve a community, and if that community is not thriving, a library will not thrive.

How do we demonstrate, in more than just words, our commitment to the sustainability of those who work in our libraries, use our libraries, live in our community, and reside on this planet?

Our sustainability is nested within the community's sustainability—however you choose to define *community*.

NOTES

1. Michael E. Porter, *Competitive Strategy: Techniques for Analyzing Industries and Competitors* (New York: Free Press, 1998).
2. David Lankes, "Library as Platform: Unlocking the Potential of Our Communities" (webinar), August 15, 2012, https://davidlankes.org/library-as-platform-unlocking-the-potential-of-our-communities/.

DEEP DIVE: MISSION STATEMENT

Write out your library's current mission statement:

_____

_____

_____

_____

_____

_____

_____

_____

_____

_____

_____

_____

_____

_____

Reflect on that mission statement. Does it speak to helping your community thrive? To bounce back from disruption? If not, how could it be better?

_____

_____

_____

_____

_____

_____

_____

_____

_____

_____

_____

_____

_____

_____

_____

THE WHY BEHIND THE WHAT

WHY DO SOME BRANDS INSPIRE INTENSE LOYALTY AND others do not? Why do some libraries thrive while others wither on the vine?

In his best-selling book *Start with Why,* author and business consultant Simon Sinek seeks to answer the question of how some companies inspire intense brand loyalty. As most consultants do, Sinek uses pattern recognition: he watches for commonalities among successful businesses and shared characteristics of businesses that do not do as well as others. Through his work he identified a pattern found among successful businesses and well-known public figures. He calls this pattern "The Golden Circle" and represents it in the diagram shown in figure 7.1.

Given the title of Sinek's book, you can likely see where this explanation will begin. Those companies that craft messaging and publicity for themselves and their products that speak to why they do what they do before they talk about how or what they do garner more support in the marketplace.

The pattern reveals that, in a flooded marketplace, people buy *why* a company does what it does more than *what* it does. This revelation matches up with research provided in the seminal 2008 OCLC report, *From Awareness to Funding: A Study of Library Support in America,* which revealed that those voters most likely to vote yes for a budget increase for libraries are not our users, they are our philosophical supporters, people

FIGURE 7.1 ──────────────────────────────────

SIMON SINEK'S GOLDEN CIRCLE

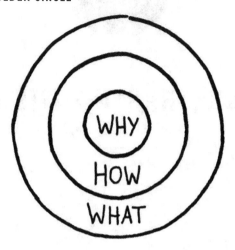

who *believe* in what libraries stand for, not so much for what happens to be on the library's program calendar this year.[1]

Let's walk through the Golden Circle together to make sure we can equate it to libraries:

1. Why: This is the core belief of the organization. It is why the organization exists.
2. How: This is how the organization fulfills that core belief.
3. What: This is what the organization does to fulfill that core belief.

The Golden Circle reveals that messaging and publicity that start with why you do something are more impactful than a laundry list of what you do. Why you do something will resonate with users and nonusers alike. Why you do something should tug on the heartstrings, speak to the inner desires of a person, connect with people's values so that they see their hopes and aspirations for themselves or others reflected back to them.

Sinek provides the following example:

> I use Apple because they are easy to understand and everybody gets
> it. If Apple were like everyone else, a marketing message from them
> might sound like this: "We make great computers. They're beauti-
> fully designed, simple to use, and user friendly. Want to buy one?"
>
> "Meh."
>
> And that's how most of us communicate. That's how most mar-
> keting is done, that's how most sales are done, and that's how most
> of us communicate interpersonally. We say what we do, we say how
> we are different or how we are better, and we expect some sort of
> behavior—a purchase or vote or something like that. "Here's our
> new law firm. We have the best lawyers with the biggest clients.
> We always perform for our clients—do business with us." "Here's
> our new car—it gets great gas mileage, it has leather seats—buy
> our car." But it's uninspiring.
>
> Here's how Apple actually communicates. *"Everything we do, we
> believe in challenging the status quo, we believe in thinking differently.*
> The way we challenge the status quo is by making our products
> beautifully designed, simple to use, and user friendly. We just happen
> to make great computers. Want to buy one?"
>
> Totally different, right? You're ready to buy a computer from
> me. All I did was reverse the order of the information. . . . People
> don't buy what you do, people buy why you do it.[2]

In the Apple example, we see a message that starts with why: we believe
in challenging the status quo. Think back to when Apple launched the
Macintosh computer. It was with the company's Super Bowl commercial, "1984." Images in the commercial alluded to George Orwell's novel,
1984, which described a dystopian future ruled by "Big Brother." In the
commercial a subservient audience is watching a talking head on a large
screen when a strong, beautiful female athlete runs through the audience,
toward the screen, carrying a sledgehammer while wearing a tank top with
the Apple logo on it. She smashes the screen, the audience is startled, and
the closing comments announce the arrival of the Macintosh computer.

This message—we're here to free you from assumptions about the way
your computer has to be, we're here to challenge the status quo—resonated

with baby boomers who had come up in the 1960s and were all about being radical and not becoming "The Man." It also coincided with this generation's growing amount of disposable income. When the boomers looked at where to buy a home computer, they felt connected to a company that represented their worldview; they were, or wanted to be, all about breaking the mold. Their money went to a company that represented how they wanted to see themselves.

Another excellent example in *Start with Why* is that of Dr. Martin Luther King Jr. Sinek noted that Dr. King's ability to speak with conviction about his civil and human rights beliefs, about his vision for the future of America, was key to the rallying of the civil rights movement. That because he could articulate his passion for a brighter future for all Americans, regardless of the color of their skin, he encouraged a following that also had a passion for a brighter future for themselves and their fellow Americans. He did not say "I have a plan" for the future of civil and human rights in America; he eloquently delivered an impassioned speech that used the phrase "I have a dream" over and over. The power of those words is felt to this day because Dr. King spoke with energy, conviction, and solidarity with the dreams of millions of others who wanted things to change in our country. *That's* how you do it.

My mentor, Josh Cohen, the former director of the Mid-Hudson Library System, once said to me that leaders are just people who articulate how you feel better than you can. There's a lot of truth to that in my experience.

To be seen and respected as a leader in your community, you, and your library, need to get really good at articulating your community's vision for the future. Then you can talk about how the library will contribute to that vision and what, specifically, you do to bring that vision to life.

How well does your library articulate why you do what you do?

When I think of the "why behind the what" for libraries, I think of the Core Values list from the American Library Association:

- Access
- Confidentiality/Privacy
- Democracy
- Diversity
- Education and Lifelong Learning

- Intellectual Freedom
- Preservation
- The Public Good
- Professionalism
- Service
- Social Responsibility

These values speak to what the world is looking for today from public institutions. There might be a particular flavor of these items that best reflects the hopes and aspirations of your particular community, but the roots of everything that we need in order to have a message that connects are right here in this list of values.

How we carry out these values may look slightly, or a lot, different depending on the community served, but the values themselves remain steady throughout economic, societal, political, technological, and environmental changes. These are our "whys." This is why we do what we do.

The particulars of what we do must be set in the context of our local community, and we'll talk more about that later in the book, but the intent and the messaging behind what we do and how we do it are right here. The core values just listed are a rock-solid reference point that provides guidance when times are tough: when you're constructing advocacy messages to make the case for funding or when you've just witnessed what the human digestive system is capable of in the library's restroom—sometimes you just need a reminder of what this profession is all about.

What if we were to consistently talk about the why behind what we do instead of just the what? What if we got incredibly good at talking about our core values? What if all publicity about the library included the reminder that libraries are about empowering those we serve? That libraries are about ensuring access to information and education for all, not just those who can pay? That libraries are a cornerstone of a democracy? That a free people cannot truly be free without access to the information and services offered by the modern public library? What if we routinely reminded people that we are intellectual freedom fighters? That libraries are on the front lines of defending public access to information in all formats, from all viewpoints, and while we're at it, we're one of the few organizations in modern life that is working to protect your privacy. **We are a force for good.**

What do all these values add up to? In my opinion, they all add up to "life, liberty, and the pursuit of happiness." That is something almost all Americans can get behind. However, we find ourselves in a time in history when politics, the media, and corporations have lined up to make us feel that our lives, liberties, and happiness are infringed upon, threatened by, or reduced by "others." This framing of our society keeps us at odds, keeps us watching the news to see what will negatively impact our lives next, keeps us rooting for politicians who we think will represent our worldview, keeps us suspicious of our neighbors.

But what if someone was the champion of us all? An institution that wasn't out to profit from dissent and mistrust? An institution that values education and intellectual freedom for all? And what if that institution (hint: libraries), which already was doing these things, *was actually widely recognized as such?*

What if we distilled our work and messaging down to the idea that everything we do, every choice we make as institutions, every service we design, every program we offer, all the technology we deploy—all of it—is to add to the greater good? To help sustain our communities, whether we define *community* as local or global.

Take some time to assess what messages your library is sending using the worksheet at the end of this chapter. Put on the hat of an outsider, someone unfamiliar with your library. Is there a message? Is it cohesive? Do the work. You might be surprised at what you are telling the world, or not telling the world.

What if, like the West Vancouver Memorial Library, we adopt the core value of sustainability for our institutions?

The West Vancouver (British Columbia) Memorial Library first formally adopted sustainability as a core value in its 2010–2015 Strategic Plan:

> Sustainability: We manage our resources responsibly to enhance our
> financial stability, social goodwill, and environmental leadership.

Then the library evolved. In its 2016–2020 Strategic Plan, the library once again adopted sustainability as a core value but turned the phrase outward:

Sustainability: We manage our resources responsibly to maintain financial, social, and environmental sustainability for the well-being of our community.

The West Vancouver Memorial Library went from being focused on the library's sustainability to being focused on the community's sustainability.

This outlook is at the heart of sustainable thinking for libraries. If we manage and deploy our resources—from our staff and facilities to our services and programs—with an eye toward sustainability, we strengthen not only ourselves but our communities. That is a message that will inspire people of all walks of life to invest in our institutions.

Here's the truth: most people outside the library profession (and, unfortunately, some still in the profession) have lost sight of why libraries do what they do. Most people barely know *what* we do, let alone why and how we do these things.

We need to get better at talking about *why,* or a decline in investment is exactly what will happen.

NOTES

1. Cathy De Rosa and Jenny Johnson, *From Awareness to Funding: A Study of Library Support in America* (Dublin, OH: OCLC, 2008).
2. Simon Sinek, "How Great Leaders Inspire Action," TED Talk, September 2009, TED.com.

WHAT MESSAGE ARE YOU SENDING?

Take a few moments to click through your library's website.
- Look at the program calendar.
- Check out your library's press releases, newsletters, and annual report to the community.

- Visit the resources page and review the itemized listing of technology, databases, and e-resources that you offer.
- Check out the "About" section.

If you were not a library user, would you understand why the library offers what it does from a collection, program, and services perspective?

_____

_____

_____

What is the core message your library is sending?

_____

_____

_____

Critically review your library's website:
- Does your library's mission statement reflect a commitment to building a better world?
- Does your annual report to the community tie what you did to why you did it?
- Do program descriptions make the connection between the program's topic and the outcome your library is trying to achieve by offering that program?

_____

_____

_____

WHY
CORE VALUES OF LIBRARIANSHIP

Access / Confidentiality/Privacy / Democracy / Diversity /
Education and Lifelong Learning / Intellectual Freedom / Preservation /
The Public Good / Professionalism / Service / Social Responsibility
—CORE VALUES OF LIBRARIANSHIP, AMERICAN LIBRARY ASSOCIATION

WHY DO WE DO WHAT WE DO? I BET YOU ASK YOURSELF this question every now and again. Particularly after a rough day at the library. We can sometimes lose sight of our calling in the everyday. This makes it critical that you connect with your *personal* why—why do you do what you do in the library profession? Why do you believe libraries matter? Can you articulate *your* why? This is the first step to connecting with more people who may need your services or who may need to take action to ensure that your library is viable for the long haul.

I am a well-intentioned World War II history buff. If you are not a fan of the book or miniseries *Band of Brothers,* let me fill you in about my favorite part of the miniseries: an episode called "Why We Fight" reminds me how critical it is to keep our "why" front and center. The story of *Band of Brothers* follows a parachute infantry company in the 101st Airborne Division in the European Theater during World War II. From jump training at Camp Toccoa in Georgia to D-Day, through Holland, to the Siege of Bastogne, this story is, and mostly seems focused on, a depiction of men at war and the camaraderie that is born out of going into battle together. However, in "Why We Fight," the *why behind the what* emerges.

This portion of the story is an account of the liberation of a sub-camp of Dachau, the Kaufering concentration camp. Although some liberties were taken in storytelling to put the characters of the story at this particular camp at that particular moment, the point of what the soldiers encounter is not lost. The soldiers see, firsthand, for the first time after months of grueling battle, the treatment of Jews, Poles, Russians, French, and outsiders by German society.

In the shared moments of loss, grief, horror, and perseverance between the soldiers and the prisoners of the concentration camp, things come into focus—this is why we, as a society, should fight, why soldiers risk everything, why we speak out against intolerance and discrimination, why ideas need to be open, discussed, and debated.

This moment in the miniseries always reminds me that **libraries are part of keeping the world a sane place**. That if we want peace on Earth, education, civil civic dialogue, and democracy, then we have to work at it every day.

Our work in libraries speaks to this—the promotion of understanding, empathy, and respect for our fellow citizens. This is a responsibility we cannot take lightly, for even on those days when a patron is on your last nerve or the printer has another paper jam, it truly is all for a higher calling, something we need to work hard to promote and to be proud of.

If, like me, you have not taken the time to read the American Library Association's Core Values of Librarianship in some time, please do. They are listed at the beginning of this chapter and in the following paragraphs. Take a moment, read through them, and reflect on how what you read here speaks to why you do the work you do for those whom you serve at your library. Then use the worksheet "What's Your Why?" at the end of this chapter to work on articulating why you believe in our profession. After I recently read these core values again, they helped me boil down my why: because I believe in life, liberty, and the pursuit of happiness—for all.

Access

All information resources that are provided directly or indirectly by the library, regardless of technology, format, or methods of delivery, should be readily, equally, and equitably accessible to all library users. (ALA Policy Manual B.2.1.15 Economic Barriers to Information Access)

Confidentiality/Privacy

Protecting user privacy and confidentiality is necessary for intellectual freedom and fundamental to the ethics and practice of librarianship. (ALA Policy Manual B.2.1.17 Privacy)

Democracy

A democracy presupposes an informed citizenry. The First Amendment mandates the right of all persons to free expression, and the corollary right to receive the constitutionally protected expression of others. The publicly supported library provides free and equal access to information for all people of the community the library serves. (Interpretations of the Library Bill of Rights; Economic Barriers to Information Access)

Diversity

We value our nation's diversity and strive to reflect that diversity by providing a full spectrum of resources and services to the communities we serve. (ALA Policy Manual B.3 Diversity; Libraries: An American Value)

Education and Lifelong Learning

ALA promotes the creation, maintenance, and enhancement of a learning society, encouraging its members to work with educators, government officials, and organizations in coalitions to initiate and support comprehensive efforts to ensure that school, public, academic, and special libraries in every community cooperate to provide lifelong learning services to all. (ALA Policy Manual A.1.1 Introduction)

Intellectual Freedom

We uphold the principles of intellectual freedom and resist all efforts to censor library resources. (ALA Policy Manual B.2 Intellectual Freedom; ALA Code of Ethics, Article II)

The Public Good

ALA reaffirms the following fundamental values of libraries in the context of discussing outsourcing and privatization of library services. These values include that libraries are an essential public good and are fundamental institutions in democratic societies. (1998–99 CD #24.1, Motion #1)

Preservation

The Association supports the preservation of information published in all media and formats. The association affirms that the preservation of information resources is central to libraries and librarianship. (ALA Policy Manual B.8.3 Preservation, Preservation Policy)

Professionalism

The American Library Association supports the provision of library services by professionally qualified personnel who have been educated in graduate programs within institutions of higher education. It is of vital importance that there be professional education available to meet the social needs and goals of library services. (ALA Policy Manual B.7.1 Graduate Programs in Library and Information Studies)

Service

We provide the highest level of service to all library users. We strive for excellence in the profession by maintaining and enhancing our own knowledge and skills, by encouraging the professional development of co-workers, and by fostering the aspirations of potential members of the profession. (ALA Code of Ethics)

Social Responsibility

ALA recognizes its broad social responsibilities. The broad social responsibilities of the American Library Association are defined in terms of the contribution that librarianship can make in ameliorating or solving the critical problems of society; support for efforts to help inform and educate the people of the United States on these problems and to encourage them to examine the many views on and the facts regarding each problem; and the willingness of ALA to take a position on current critical issues with the relationship to libraries and library service set forth in the position statement. (ALA Policy Manual A.1.1 Mission, Priority Areas, Goals)

WHAT'S YOUR WHY?

Choose one of the core values and write a personal value statement. Can you get your personal value statement down to one sentence? Conveying your *why* succinctly is key to communicating with stakeholders inside and outside your library.

_____

_____

_____

_____

_____

_____

_____

_____

_____

_____

_____

HOW

THE THREE ES OF SUSTAINABLE LIBRARIES

IN *START WITH WHY*, THE SECOND RING WITHIN THE
Golden Circle is "How." If we agree that our *why* is where we start, the
next layer to define is *how* we carry out those things we find on the Core
Values of Librarianship list. How do we provide access? Strengthen democracy? Promote lifelong learning? And something that should probably be
added to the Core Values list: co-create sustainable communities?

An interpretation of the word *sustainability* that we will talk more about
in a later chapter is the *triple bottom line* of sustainability, encompassing
not just environmentally appropriate responses but economic and socially
equitable responses as well. This approach is sometimes called the Three
Es: *environment, economics,* and *social equity.* It is frequently described as
the "three-legged stool," the idea being that if all three are not equally
addressed, the stool will tip over and therefore be unsustainable.

I propose that *how* we carry out our work in libraries is also a three-
legged stool encompassing Three Es: *Empower, Engage, and Energize.* All
three need to be present to create a sustainable library.

It's a two-way street: A library can empower its patrons to go forth
and do good things by engaging with them to understand their hopes
and aspirations. A community can see and feel the authentic interest a
library has in being a part of that community's conversations and sees the
library at the table, or convening "the table," to find community-based

solutions. When a library does the work to engage with its community and show love and support for the goals and aspirations of those it serves by empowering and energizing patrons through library services, those communities turn around and give empowerment right back to their library in the form of goodwill and financial investment. This is a sustainable pattern for the future of libraries.

Inside the library:

- *Empower:* All stakeholders are empowered to make the library the best that it can be, to find solutions, to own problems, and to step up when necessary.
- *Engage:* All stakeholders—staff, board, and the community—feel respected and are included as part of the team that is making the library a success.
- *Energize:* All stakeholders are enthused about the library and where it is going as an organization and, as a result, bring that energy to the work, to the board table, and to community interactions.

With our community:

- *Empower:* Community members are empowered to take control of their lives and the lives of their children and to make their neighborhood a better place through access to information and programs provided by the library.
- *Engage:* Community members think of the library as "theirs" and are engaged with the library board and Friends group or are passionately supportive of the role the library plays in the community.
- *Energize:* Community members feel energized by the library and share that energy back to make the library and community better.

A community that is empowered, engaged, and energized will envelop the library in the community's lifestyle, consider the library to be a part of the community, and interface with the library in ways that make it part of the neighborhood. Community members own it, want to see it continue and thrive, and rely on the sustainability of our capacity to serve them.

We, as libraries, do not exist without them, the members of the community. Are we contributing more than "stuff"? Are we empowering those we come into contact with to truly have a better life?

At home, at work, and in our communities, we are all looking for a place to belong, to contribute, to improve the world around us. We quest for happiness at the personal, professional, and civic levels.

> Martin Seligman, one of the leading researchers in positive psychology and author of *Authentic Happiness,* describes happiness as having three parts: *pleasure, engagement,* and *meaning* [italics added]. Pleasure is the "feel good" part of happiness. Engagement refers to living a "good life" of work, family, friends, and hobbies. Meaning refers to using our strengths to contribute to a larger purpose. Seligman says that all three are important, but that of the three, engagement and meaning make the most difference to living a happy life. ("What Is Happiness?" http://thisemotionallife.org/topic/happiness/what-happiness)

John Cotton Dana, often considered the father of modern libraries, once said, "The public library is a center of public happiness first, of public education next."

Happiness is an "unalienable" right in the United States, listed in the Declaration of Independence right next to life and liberty. It is a core value of the founding of our country and something that is proven to make the world a better place. Does your library respect and reflect that?

Multiple studies on depression and happiness have revealed that giving to others, doing for others, is a key to satisfaction and happiness in life. Money spent to benefit someone other than ourselves has been found to be more psychologically rewarding than buying items for ourselves.[1] This truth speaks to the idea, shared in chapter 3, of self-transcendence—thinking beyond ourselves and keeping the greater good at the core of our actions.

A library that reflects the Three Es of a Sustainable Library works to create an experience-based library, where users are part of program and service design, where library science is applied to real life to effect positive change, and where happiness is an actual, acceptable outcome to measure success. Use the "Power to the People" worksheet at the end of this chapter to identify how your library empowers your community members to make the library theirs.

Take a look at the following three examples to get a sense of what this approach can, and does, look like:

- **Camp Happiness**
  At the 2014 Public Library Association (PLA) conference in Indianapolis, Indiana, I had the pleasure of wandering into "Camp Happiness" on the exhibit floor. Modeled on the Rangeview Library District's Experience Zone project called the "Happiness Experience," the space evoked a sense of calm and had a variety of stations at which we could do something or engage with the space in a way that brought happiness to the fore. Colorado's Rangeview Library District, perhaps better known as "Anythink," one of the most innovative and forward-thinking libraries in the world, had developed the Happiness Experience in 2012 as part of the library's goal to create twelve Experience Zones: *"a place/space in the library where our guests could engage with information, learn something new, do something hands-on and hopefully leave with something tangible."*[2] At the PLA iteration of Camp Happiness, there was scientific information about happiness, aromatherapy items, postcards to send a positive message to a loved one, and wooden tokens with pay-it-forward prompts: "Give a compliment," "Share your space," "Help hold the door." We were encouraged to complete these tasks and then pass on the wooden token so that happiness would continue to spread beyond the conference doors.

- **Library Takeover: Make [*Your Idea Here*] Happen at Your Library**
  After a concerted effort to hear from segments of the community that were least represented in the public libraries through a "Tell Us" in-person survey campaign, the Madison (Wisconsin) Public Library (MPL) partnered with the Madison Public Library Foundation to create a community-driven framework for developing adult programming. Library Takeover invited applications from teams of three to five community members, not affiliated with a nonprofit or institution, to create their own large-scale events using their library as the platform. The initial Takeover program received thirty-nine applications! Three teams were chosen, and the program provided a

six-week event-planning boot camp with local experts to help team members plan their events. The events produced included a dance party preceded by a discussion on the ways that nightlife spaces can be inaccessible to members of the community; a gathering of local poets, writers, spoken-word performers, hip-hop artists, and storytellers that brought the Madison writing community together; and a celebration of local Indian American culture that attracted more than four hundred people. "It's about publicly and loudly committing library resources—whatever those may be—so that community members have an opportunity to host their own events," said Laura Damon-Moore, community engagement librarian at MPL at a discussion session at the 2017 American Library Association Annual Conference.

- **Community as Collection**
  The School of Information Studies (iSchool) at Syracuse University has received a National Leadership Grant from the Institute of Museum and Library Services to create a workflow for libraries to assess community learning needs; identify community experts' interests and availability to offer their expertise; and build data models to capture needs and people resources as a "collection" of human resources based at the libraries. This idea extends the popular Human Library or "human book" program idea, in which program attendees get to "check a neighbor out of the library" to have a conversation, and creates a lasting community database of expertise that is surfaced and accessible. The goal of the Syracuse project is to develop a workflow process for librarians to catalog, coordinate, and promote that collective expertise. This program celebrates the wisdom of local experts and helps connect neighbors with neighbors, perfectly exemplifying the idea that to be resilient we need to know one another and work together.

NOTES

1. Kathryn E. Buchanan and Anat Bardi, "Acts of Kindness and Acts of Novelty Affect Life Satisfaction," *Journal of Social Psychology* 150, no. 3 (2010), www.tandfonline.com/doi/abs/10.1080/00224540903365554.

2. Justina Wooten, "Made Happy at Camp Happiness," *Anythink* (blog), March 27, 2014, https://www.anythinklibraries.org/blog/made-happy-camp-happiness.

POWER TO THE PEOPLE

How is your community empowered to help shape services and programs at your library?

_____

_____

_____

_____

_____

_____

_____

_____

_____

_____

_____

_____

_____

WHAT
LOCAL SUPPORTS LOCAL

WE'VE IDENTIFIED OUR *WHY* BY EMBEDDING OUR WORK in our core values. We've taken a look at *how* we carry out our values with the Three Es of Sustainable Libraries. The truth is, to manifest the two-way street of the Three Es of Sustainable Libraries, you need to carry out programs and services that connect with your local community. That empowerment, engagement, and energy exchange isn't going to happen without generating intense local loyalty to your library through programs and services that matter to *your* community.

That **intense local loyalty** to your library is what will translate into the outcomes you've always dreamed of—happy, healthy residents and taxpayers willing to speak up for and reinvest in your library.

I can't tell you what to do because I don't know your community. That's your work: to get out there and listen. Identify your community's hopes for the future and then apply library science to help them create the future they are dreaming of.

We've all heard the phrase *"Think global, act local."* The inspiration for that phrase has been traced to a Scottish town planner and social activist, Patrick Geddes, in his 1915 book *Cities in Evolution*. Geddes believed in working with the environment rather than working against it:

Adapted and expanded from my article "Local Supports Local," *Library Journal,* July 11, 2016 (http://lj.libraryjournal.com/2016/07/lj-in-print/local-supports-local-sustainability/#_).

> "Local character" is thus no mere accidental old-world quaintness, as its mimics think and say. It is attained only in course of adequate grasp and treatment of the whole environment, and in active sympathy with the essential and characteristic life of the place concerned.

The local economy. The local ecosystem. Local food. Local arts. Local history. Local *everything*. As we strategize our unique value position for the future, nothing is more unique than *our* local. Each town, campus, school that has a library is unique and has a culture and environment of its own that needs to be cultivated, preserved, and celebrated. Who better to tap into that ethos than the library?

> Localism is grounded in the belief that relationships matter, most. The way we interact with where we live—who we do business with—how we connect with people, other life, the land—all of it matters. (Business Alliance for Local Living Economies, https://bealocalist.org/what-is-localism/)

In the 2013 documentary *Crafting a Nation,* local craft brewers, restaurateurs, and large-scale brewers who have decided to open up operations in Asheville, North Carolina, speak to the vibrancy of Asheville and identify a key ingredient of why Asheville works: the commitment to "localism." They note that money spent in local businesses gets reinvested into the community—again and again.

Thanks to a Civic Economics study for Local First in Grand Rapids, Michigan,[1] we know the following:

- For every $100 spent at a locally owned business, $73 remains in the local economy and $27 leaves. Compare that to the same $100 spent at a non–locally owned business, where $43 remains in the local economy and $57 leaves.
- Local eateries return nearly 79 percent of revenues to the community, compared to just over 30 percent for chain restaurants.
- A 10 percent shift in market share from chains to local businesses could result in nearly $140 million in new economic activity, more than 1,600 new jobs, and more than $50 million in new wages.

According to the U.S. Small Business Administration, small businesses "accounted for 65 percent (or 9.8 million) of the 15 million net new jobs created between 1993 and 2009."[2] More jobs in your town mean more people, more businesses, and more tax dollars for your community to benefit from.

Sue Lynn Sasser, PhD and professor of economics at the University of Central Oklahoma, has quoted studies showing that nonprofits receive 250 percent more support from small businesses than from large ones.[3] That is some hard evidence that local supports local!

The Business Alliance for Local Living Economies defines *localism* as "building communities that are more healthy and sustainable—backed by local economies that are stronger and more resilient."

In addition to the local economy, the triple bottom line approach to sustainability guides us to understand and respect the importance of the local environment and the equitability of the local social fabric. This awareness opens the door for the library to use its resources, services, and influence in ways that speak to the tenets of sustainable thinking for the future of libraries—contributing to not only sustainable but resilient and regenerative communities.

Think back to number 9 on the Resilient Design Institute's list of Resilient Design Principles (chapter 5): "*Social equity and community contribute to resilience.* Strong, culturally diverse communities in which people know, respect, and care for each other will fare better during times of stress or disturbance. Social aspects of resilience can be as important as physical responses." This principle should be at the heart of what libraries do: **strengthening the social fabric** so that we can support one another where we live, work, learn, and love.

How do you do this? The American Library Association's "turning outward" resources available through the Libraries Transforming Communities (LTC) initiative are brilliant at supporting your efforts in this area. The resources include simple tools such as the *Ask Exercise* and the *Community Conversation Workbook* to help facilitate the market research you will need to do in order to engage with your community and learn more about how community members see everyone working together to create a more sustainable, resilient community. The program may be better named Communities Transforming Libraries because that concept is at the heart of the work we need to do: community-influenced design of programs and services is the outcome of the work you will do with ALA's free "turning outward" tool kit.

When thinking about who you will talk to using the "turning outward" tools, it is critical that you come into contact with a wide cross section of the community. Ensure that you are not talking only to library users. Get out there and map your community. Think through various demographic categories such as age, income level, educational background; the geography of the area that your library serves; the length of time a resident has lived in your area; and political affiliation.

Cross-reference the preceding information with the various stakeholder and influencer groups in your community:

- Municipal leaders
- Emergency services providers (police, firefighters, EMTs)
- School district leadership (administrators, teachers, building and grounds staff, parent-teacher association members)
- Small-business owners
- Nonprofit and religious organization leaders

Use this chapter's worksheet, "Small-Business Inventory," to take a deep dive into your small-business community. There may be a number of small shops that you've never personally come across that are contributing to the local economy.

Key individuals to speak with will emerge quickly. Design your process to include the opportunity to speak with everyday people who might be under the radar of traditional input-seeking activities. If you don't know someone personally, don't let that stop you from reaching out. Your recognition of an individual's important position in the community—even if the person is "just a resident" and doesn't hold a traditional leadership role in the community—will go a long way toward helping that individual understand that the library is for everyone and is working to be a part of solutions that will build a stronger, more sustainable community.

An intriguing alternative, built on the chassis of "Turning Outward," is the Madison (Wisconsin) Public Library's Tell Us/Cuéntenos Campaign. This library wanted to engage with its community with as few barriers in place as possible. Study designers challenged traditional public feedback tools and avoided a prescriptive method or "anything with checkboxes." Drawing from deliberative dialogue methods, the library designed a decentralized strategy to help focus on the community's most vulnerable populations.

> Using equity as a goal and guide for all our decisions, we used a combination of anecdotal, qualitative and quantitative information about local demographic dynamics and issues in public libraries to identify the communities least represented in our libraries and in our city. ("Communities Inspiring Libraries: A Strategic Plan for Eastside Growth," Madison [Wisconsin] Public Library)

The library developed a booklet that allowed any resident to conduct a kitchen table–style conversation: the booklet contained an introduction, instructions, questions, and prompts for the note-taker with minimal demographic and contact fields. The booklet was designed to contain the notes from the conversation and came in its own self-addressed envelope for easy return. Participants held conversations at a variety of venues, from people's homes to classrooms, libraries, community centers, and workspaces. The library obtained the following results:

- Fifty-two conversations among 338 participants
- Of those participants, 50 percent were library cardholders
- Average age was 32 (with a range from 8 to 84)

When local supports local, you build a community together. When you build something together, you want to see it succeed, and you will work to plan for the long haul. When you know your neighbors, it is easier to support each other in good times and in times of crisis and need. Libraries need to be a part of that conversation and the localism movement in bigger and more obvious ways.

If you think you do this already and it isn't paying dividends, then you're doing it wrong. For libraries that issue "community surveys" at the front desk and call it a day or leave flyers with the elementary school secretary and then put a checkmark next to "outreach to local school" on their to-do list, that isn't cutting it. Our profession needs to seriously step up our game when it comes to not just "outreach" but connection and engagement with those we truly serve—not just those who walk through the doors of the library building.

The library's support of local is a strategic message that needs to be amplified from your institution. This is part of being deliberate and "unique." We often assume that people know who we are and what we're all about, but honestly, nothing could be farther from the truth. Most Americans don't understand the modern library. They think we are likely good people doing good work, but they often confuse the library with a book warehouse.

We are education. We are essential to the communities that we serve. Framing our messages to highlight why we do what we do and why it matters is critical to our sustainability in the future. This process starts with listening. Not guessing. Not assuming. Not speaking down from on high. Start by humanely asking good questions, like the ones you'll find through the LTC program, and truly listen before you jump to design solutions that you think fit the perceived need. Gather intel. Build a profile of the community using the trend information you gather.

When you deeply understand the hopes and dreams of the community you serve, you can design services, programs, and, most important, *partnerships* that inspire your community members to invest their goodwill and finances in the library.

Build intense local loyalty to your library. Be laser focused on your community members and what matters to them. Only you can discover that, act on it, and ensure that your library is part of the social fabric of the lives of your community members and vice versa.

NOTES

1. Erica Fetherston, "Local Works! Examining the Impact of Local Business on the West Michigan Economy," Local First Arizona, September 15, 2008, https://www.localfirstaz .com/news/local-works-michigan-study.

2. "Frequently Asked Questions," Small Business Administration, Office of Advocacy, https://www.sba.gov/sites/default/files/sbfaq.pdf.

3. Brooke Barnett, "15 Reasons to Shop Locally," *MetroFamily Magazine,* February 2013, www.metrofamilymagazine.com/February-2013/15-Reasons-to-Shop-Locally/.

SMALL-BUSINESS INVENTORY

Map the small-business community in your town. List the name of each business and the name of the business owner(s). Then indicate whether you know the owners personally or, if not, who you know that knows them. Note whether your library has interacted with this business in the past and how you might better support the business in the future.

BUSINESS NAME	OWNER(S)	WHO YOU KNOW	NOTES

SUSTAINABLE THINKING
DEFINED

SUSTAINABLE THINKING, AS INTRODUCED EARLIER IN THIS book, brings together all the things we have been talking about.

The American Library Association's 2015 Resolution on the Importance of Sustainable Libraries, modeled on the 2014 resolution passed by the New York Library Association, provides the case statement:

> *Whereas* our communities are faced with economic, environmental, and societal changes that are of great concern to our quality of life;
>
> *Whereas* libraries are uniquely positioned and essential to build the capacity of the communities they serve to become sustainable, resilient and regenerative;
>
> *Whereas* library leaders, and those who inspire future library leaders, have a mandate to ensure future access to economical library services;
>
> *Whereas* libraries that demonstrate good stewardship of the resources entrusted to them can build community support that leads to sustainable funding;

Whereas the people who work in our libraries and those who access services in our facilities deserve a healthy environment in which to do so;

Whereas the Intergovernmental Panel on Climate Change (IPCC) has determined that: "Human influence on the climate system is clear. . . . Recent climate changes have had widespread impacts on human and natural systems";

Whereas the American Library Association has acknowledged in its 2015 Strategic Plan that "Libraries are widely recognized as key players in economic development, in building strong and vibrant communities, and in sustaining a strong democracy" and launched the ALA Center for Civic Life (CCL) in 2010 in conjunction with the Kettering Foundation to promote community engagement and foster public deliberation through libraries; and

Whereas libraries that demonstrate leadership in making sustainable decisions that positively address climate change, respect and use natural resources, and create healthy indoor and outdoor environments will stabilize and reduce their long-term energy costs, help build more sustainable communities, and thereby increase community support for the library; now, therefore, be it

Resolved, that the American Library Association (ALA), on behalf of its members:

- recognizes the important and unique role libraries play in wider community conversations about resiliency, climate change, and a sustainable future and begins a new era of thinking sustainably in order to consider the economic, environmental, and socially equitable viability of choices made on behalf of the association;
- enthusiastically encourages activities by itself, its membership, library schools, and state associations to be proactive in their application of sustainable thinking in the areas of facilities,

operations, policy, technology, programming, partnerships, and library school curricula; and

- directs the ALA Executive Director to pursue sustainable choices when planning conferences and meetings and to actively promote best practices of sustainability through ALA publications, research, and educational opportunities to reach our shared goal of vital, visible, and viable libraries for the future.

Adopted by the Council of the American Library Association
Sunday, June 28, 2015, in San Francisco, California

Sustainable thinking refers to the alignment of a library's core values and resources—which can mean staff time and energy, facilities, collections, and technology—with the local and global community's right to endure, bounce back from disruption, and thrive by bringing new and energetic life to fruition through choices made in all areas of library operations and outreach. This definition is a call to action for libraries of all types to think differently, with intent, about everything that we do.

Seth Godin, an American author, entrepreneur, and marketer, declared in 2012 that **"the map has been replaced by the compass."** He noted that it doesn't pay to memorize the route because the route will change. The compass, on the other hand, is more important than ever. If you don't know which direction you are going, how will you know when you are off course? Godin went on to point out that despite this reality, we spend most of our time learning (or teaching) the map, yesterday's map, while we are anxious and afraid to spend any time at all "calibrating our compass."

We need a compass setting and a way to calibrate it, a compass setting that helps to guide our operational and outreach decisions.

- *Sustainable Thinking is that compass setting.*

By placing your local and global community at the heart of your library, your path becomes much clearer. By acknowledging that the world is changing around us, we may need to adjust accordingly to be resilient. We create a culture of Sustainable Thinking by putting these three tenets front and center:

- The community is at the heart of our organization.
- Disruption is constant in all sectors of life.
- Libraries can help lead the way to a better future for us all.

Your compass setting is that spot on the horizon that you are always navigating toward. Will every day bring forward motion toward that spot? No. But if all the small things you do regularly add up to that compass setting, you're steering your library on a course that will matter—a course that, along the way, will help you build a viable, visible, and vital library that is doing good work while inspiring investment.

- *Sustainable Thinking asks you to put people first, in the most basic of ways.*
- *Thinking sustainably is a way to live our values out loud.*

Not all marketing and publicity is verbal or written. Telling our story is as much, if not more, about our actions than about press releases and viral social media marketing.

Sustainability, the capacity to endure, is vital not only for the organizational development goal of ensuring access to library services for the long haul but also for the environment. This principle is at the core of sustainable thinking. If we strategically choose to be "sustainable," we will need to layer this message into all we do.

Use the worksheet "Taking Your *Why* to the Next Level" at the end of this chapter to envision the future impact your library can have on your community if you let go of old thinking or "the way we've always done things."

The second half of this book is devoted to helping you find your path forward—providing constructions, examples, and benchmarks to work to shift that paradigm in your own mind and, I hope, in your library as well.

TAKING YOUR *WHY* TO THE NEXT LEVEL

Copy your personal *why* statement from chapter 8 here:

_____

_____

_____

_____

_____

_____

What is your vision for the impact that your library can have on your community?

_____

_____

_____

_____

_____

_____

_____

INTERPRETING SUSTAINABILITY USING THE TRIPLE BOTTOM LINE

THE WORD *SUSTAINABILITY* IS USED A LOT IN OUR WORLD. It is used when we talk about funding for our library, the environment, the capacity of an organization, the life cycle of a product. It's all over the place. And when attempting to convey an idea, it is important to have an agreed-upon interpretation of words and context.

At its simplest, sustainability is *"the capacity to endure."* Can a system, organization, process, or product continue with the current resources necessary to make it successful?

Another popular definition is from the 1987 Brundtland Commission, an international commission working on development issues for Third World countries. The Brundtland Commission's report defined sustainable development as *"development which meets the needs of current generations without compromising the ability of future generations to meet their own needs."*

But how? Like a three-year-old constantly asking why, librarians are always asking how when it comes to sustainability. There are a lot of opinions about what it takes to endure in any given situation. But a logical way to assess what it takes is provided in the triple bottom line (TBL) philosophy of sustainability. TBL is an accounting framework with three components, often referred to as the Three Es of Sustainability:

- social *equity*
- *environmental* stewardship
- *economic* feasibility

TBL accounting, as a concept, came onto the scene after the 1992 United Nations Conference on Environment and Development focused on the idea that balancing economic growth, social equity, and environmental protection was the key to sustainability. In the business world, this approach helps us consider a business's performance and impact by judging not just its bottom line of profit but also the holistic impact of the business on society, the economy, and our environment.

This acknowledgment of balance among "profit, people, and the planet" helped traditional adversaries on the topic of environmental sustainability (the business community and environmentalists) find common ground—a watershed moment in the history of our planet to be sure.

The phrase *triple bottom line* comes from the 1997 book *Cannibals with Forks: The Triple Bottom Line of 21st Century Business* by John Elkington. The title of Elkington's book comes from a question asked by Polish poet Stanislaw Jerzy Lec: "Is it progress if a cannibal uses a fork?" Elkington posits that yes, if the "cannibals" are capitalists and capitalism is here to stay, then giving them forks (the triple bottom line) will be progress.

The TBL framework goes beyond the traditional measures of profit, return on investment, and shareholder value to include environmental and social dimensions to a successful business that are beneficial to not just shareholders but stakeholders (figure 12.1). Including profits, people, and the planet to measure a company's performance has a proven track record of creating more successful business because society's value system has shifted. The current generation is not going to support a company that willfully pollutes our oceans or our air or a company that institutionalizes racism. In order for a business to be successful, it must account for all three areas—economics, environmental stewardship, and social equity—or run the risk of going out of business.

The huge focus on sustainability in the past two decades in political discourse, social media, and business strategy has come about largely thanks to the business community's awakening that "going green" and that treating workers and communities equitably do not have to decrease the bottom line.

FIGURE 12.1 —————————————————————————————————

VENN DIAGRAM DEPICTING THE DEFINITION OF THE TRIPLE BOTTOM LINE

TBL broadens the focus of an entity's responsibility beyond share-holders to *stakeholders*. In the business world, the shareholders derive a financial benefit; however, a business's stakeholders are all individuals who are influenced, directly or indirectly, by the actions of the firm: employees, customers, vendors, local residents, government agencies, and financial underwriters.

> On the face of it, shareholder value is the dumbest idea in the world. Shareholder value is a result, not a strategy . . . Your main constituencies are your employees, your customers and your products. Managers and investors should not set share price increases as their overarching goal . . . Short-term profits should be allied with an increase in the long-term value of a company.[1]

In the new way of thinking, if a tech company that builds computer hardware components is profitable but is so at the expense of the environment by harvesting raw materials until there is a scarcity of those materials and by polluting waterways in the vicinity with the wastewater from its factory requiring massive cleanups at the expense of the taxpayers, then that company's business model and our ability as a society to "afford" its product is not sustainable. The good disruption that comes from investigative journalism and citizen journalism will not keep these practices under wraps for very long.

Corporations that apply sustainable thinking to their business model can use the power of business to solve social and environmental problems and turn a profit while doing so. This realization has crystalized in a far more powerful way after the 2008 financial crisis in the United States. Companies were forced to look within to discover a long-term value proposition that consumers would actually respect and buy because the market got a lot tighter. What began to ring true was that consumers, burned by companies and business practices that put profit over people, were looking for trustworthy brands that behave ethically and have a broader worldview than the bottom line.

This perspective is being surfaced, in a big way, through the B Corporation movement. B Corporation certification is the gold standard for measuring the sustainability of a business, redefining success in business. More than fifteen thousand businesses have become certified.

> Individually, B Corps meet the highest standards of verified social and environmental performance, public transparency, and legal accountability, and aspire to use the power of markets to solve social and environmental problems.
>
> Collectively, B Corps lead a growing global movement of people using business as a force for good. Through the power of their collective voice, one day all companies will compete to be best for the world, and society will enjoy a more shared and durable prosperity for all.[2]

TBL is also making an appearance in nonprofit and government planning, supplanting the *p* for *profits* with a *p* for *policy*. Models for this approach include regional public-private collaborations such as the Wealth Creation in Rural Communities Initiative in Philadelphia, Pennsylvania; the *Community Triple Bottom Line Indicator Report* in Grand Rapids, Michigan;

and the Triple Bottom Line initiative in Cleveland, Ohio, that resulted in the passage of a law tying triple bottom line practices to local business opportunities.

Whether you refer to TBL as the "Three Ps: People, Planet, and Profit (or Policy)" or as the "Three Es: Environment, Economics, and Social Equity," the balance of the three areas is often depicted as a three-legged stool to illustrate that all three must be present in order for something, whether it be a business, a product, a policy, or a community, to be truly sustainable.

Although born in the business world to help evaluate performance with a broader perspective to create superior business value, TBL works through a variety of lenses.

You could use TBL to evaluate your community, your library, and many operational decisions made daily in your organization.

For example, a decision to purchase a product, say, summer reading program incentives, could involve the following thought process:

- Is this product affordable for the library?
- What message does this product send to the child we hand it to?
- What will become of the item when the child is done with it?

Libraries that are consciously applying sustainable thinking may soon realize that they are not living their values by buying cheap, disposable items that will never biodegrade and that are produced in an environmentally unsound manner just so a kid can get a rush of endorphins from receiving a prize for doing the right thing. More and more libraries are finding new ways to incentivize kids' summer reading—for example, helping kids see that their efforts result in matching grants from local businesses that will be donated to worthy causes can have the same desired effect on the child while helping the triple bottom line of the community.

Finding that **balance** is the challenge.

Public libraries are inherently sustainable organizations. We are coming from an organizational premise that is embedded in the sustainable mind-set.

- *Environment:* We are the forerunners of the sharing economy, creating a "borrow rather than buy" mentality for books, media, and technology—a mind-set that is expanding as we redefine what library collections can be.

- *Economics:* We produce an excellent return on investment with the dollars entrusted to us publicly and privately. The shared consumption model speaks to helping communities expand what is available to them at a low price point. Library use value calculators are a great way to help convey this fact to library users and decision makers.

- *Social Equity:* The mission of libraries is the epitome of a socially just organization. Our profession's Bill of Rights exemplifies this philosophy:

  - Books and other library resources should be provided for the interest, information, and enlightenment of all people of the community the library serves. Materials should not be excluded because of the origin, background, or views of those contributing to their creation.

  - Libraries should provide materials and information presenting all points of view on current and historical issues. Materials should not be proscribed or removed because of partisan or doctrinal disapproval.

  - A person's right to use a library should not be denied or abridged because of origin, age, background, or views. (www.ala.org/advocacy/intfreedom/librarybill)

This historic construct of a sustainable organizational doctrine positions libraries very well to embody sustainability in a much broader sense—from an organizational development perspective as well as a broader community development perspective.

As discussed earlier, true sustainability for a library is closely tied to the sustainability of its community.

TBL provides a lens through which to view our world and our institutions. TBL does not mean applying a veneer of "greenwashing" over existing practices or ensuring that the library does an Earth Day program. Sustainable Thinking is a reframing of everyday operational and outreach decisions so that the library is a model of sustainability, with an embedded eco-ethic, contributing to the creation of sustainable local and global communities.

Use the worksheet "Measure What Matters" to look at your library from four different perspectives that can help reveal where emphasis currently exists versus where it should exist.

NOTES

1. Jack Welch, quoted in Francesco Guerrera, "Welch Condemns Share Price Focus," *Financial Times,* March 12, 2009.
2. "Why B Corps Matter," B Lab, https://www.bcorporation.net/what-are-b-corps/why-b-corps-matter.
3. Robert S. Kaplan and David P. Norton, "The Balanced Scorecard—Measures That Drive Performance," *Harvard Business Review* (January-February 1992), https://hbr.org/1992/01/the-balanced-scorecard-measures-that-drive-performance-2.

MEASURE WHAT MATTERS

In "The Balanced Scorecard—Measures That Drive Performance" by Robert S. Kaplan and David P. Norton,[3] you will find the famous maxim, *"What you measure is what you get."*

Here are four questions to help you take a look at your library through multiple perspectives:

1. How do patrons see us? (customer perspective)

_____

_____

_____

_____

_____

2. What must we excel at? (internal perspective)

_____

_____

_____

_____

_____

3. Can we continue to improve and create value? (innovation and learning perspective)

_____

_____

_____

_____

_____

4. How do we look to our community? (financial perspective)

_____

_____

_____

_____

_____

WHOLE SYSTEMS
THINKING

AS JOHN MUIR, THE FAMOUS ENVIRONMENTALIST, SAID, "When we try to pick out anything by itself, we find it hitched to everything else in the Universe" (http://vault.sierraclub.org/john_muir_exhibit/writings/misquotes.aspx#2).

Near the beginning of my working life, I was an employee at a domestic violence shelter. I was, on weekends, in charge of a residence for women and children fleeing physically unsafe situations. I handled resident intake, often holding a child on my lap or doing my best not to cry as I tried to take down a mother's Social Security number and life's history and photograph any physical evidence of abuse. I quickly saw patterns that were an awakening.

I saw parents who did not graduate from high school. I saw children who had not seen a doctor regularly for wellness checkups. I saw employers that do not create a work environment accessible to single mothers. I saw schools that did not acknowledge the real-life challenges these families were faced with. I saw families that did not eat healthy foods. I saw poverty. I saw a cycle of violence that had become the norm in families.

As I would try to understand one family's situation, helping a mother find the resources she needed to make a good life for her children, I would think about what should have happened for this woman or what went wrong for her family, her community, her generation that brought her family to this point.

It was never one thing that caused a family to end up in the shelter and that felt so overwhelming to me. I'd follow one thread of a story and then realize how many issues contributed to creating this situation . . . where to begin?

My empathy streak was too wide for the work. I began to feel hopeless. I wanted to be helpful but I felt I was bailing out a sinking ocean liner with a Dixie cup. I kept wondering what it would take to lessen the number of families coming through the door of the shelter to begin with, to **systemically** address the violence that was creating an unsafe environment for these families.

When you are young, you think life is relatively simple, straightforward. That answers are binary. This is seldom the case. Although some old adages seem so simple, like "Love thy neighbor" or "Do unto others," to actually bring those adages to life in a large-scale way demands holistic thinking and deliberate action using a common compass point. Otherwise life is like a psychotic octopus—once you've got one tentacle under control, you realize seven others are wreaking havoc. As soon as you get another one under control, the one you originally thought you had figured out is now fighting with the one next to it. You will go crazy and, in some cases, do more harm than good in your efforts.

I eventually came to realize that I wanted to do work that would prevent the need for an agency like a domestic violence shelter.

Through no grand design, I landed in the library profession. At first, I didn't get the connection, but the more I learned, the more I could see the opportunity that libraries provide to maybe put a Band-Aid on today's problems and, more exciting, to mitigate or even prevent tomorrow's problems: the opportunity to help a mother when she first becomes a mother, or before she becomes a mother, or before she even knows that becoming a mother is something she will do, when she is a child; the chance to help young children understand that they are powerful, that they need to learn about the world around them, that they will help shape the world and influence those around them; the chance to provide, as Dr. David Lankes says, "a platform" for good, for learning and dialogue.

Children who learn to understand the world around them, to be inquisitive, to respect others, and to have empathy for those they may not know will grow up with a better chance of being good neighbors, great parents, and engaged citizens.

I truly believe the world has been and can continue to be changed one library at a time. Through our early literacy work, support of parents, a commitment to lifelong learning and education, digital literacy—these are just some of the ways in which we sow the seeds for a better world in the future. Libraries and librarians and library workers have never been more necessary than we are today. I say that with a pretty big caveat: this is only true if we, as a profession, recognize, respect, and live up to our own potential.

To achieve this potential, we need to become larger than ourselves, we need to think holistically and step into the roles of *catalyst, connector, and convener.*

If we are going to tackle such enormous problems as poverty, domestic violence, climate change, gender equality, clean water and air for everyone, then we need to work together. We need to engender the same value set throughout societies. We need a common goal—the health and well-being of each other. This outcome seems, at least to me, well represented in the quest for a more sustainable world when I think about sustainability through the lens of the triple bottom line (TBL).

The United Nations (UN) thinks so, too. The UN Sustainable Development Goals (figure 13.1; www.un.org/sustainabledevelopment/sustainable-development-goals/) outline the areas of work required to achieve sustainable communities:

1. No poverty
2. Zero hunger
3. Good health and well-being
4. Quality education
5. Gender equality
6. Clean water and sanitation
7. Affordable and clean energy
8. Decent work and economic growth
9. Industry, innovation, and infrastructure
10. Reduced inequalities
11. Sustainable cities and communities
12. Responsible consumption and production

FIGURE 13.1 ——————————————————————————————————
UNITED NATIONS SUSTAINABLE DEVELOPMENT GOALS

13. Climate action
14. Life below water
15. Life on land
16. Peace, justice, and strong institutions
17. Partnerships for the goals

The tasks required to reach these goals are huge, almost unfathomably huge. The job will only get easier if we pull together as a global community and harness our shared resources for such a heavy lift. Libraries have not just a role to play but a leadership role to play in all areas of these goals.

The American Library Association's Center for the Future of Libraries has identified "collective impact" as a prominent trend for libraries to respond to.

> Complex social issues—hunger, poverty, violence, education, health, public safety, the environment—involve many different factors and responses to these issues include many different community organizations. Organizations working in isolation and/or individual projects have not significantly addressed or changed many of these issues. (www.ala.org/tools/future/trends/collectiveimpact)

In a 2011 article in the *Stanford Social Innovation Review,* John Kania and Mark Kramer defined collective impact as "the commitment of a group of important actors from different sectors to a common agenda for solving a specific social problem" (https://ssir.org/articles/entry/collective_impact).

Given the enormity of the goals noted by the United Nations, the alignment of our values and resources with these goals at the macro and micro levels is a key strategy for success for our world and our libraries. The following worksheet, "Global Alignment," can help you think through, and contextualize, what you already do and could be doing toward achieving these goals.

GLOBAL ALIGNMENT

1. Read through the seventeen UN Sustainable Development Goals (www .un.org/sustainabledevelopment/sustainable-development-goals/).

2. Brainstorm:
   - What is your library already doing that helps your community in these categories?
   - What could your library be doing to help your community in these categories?

	What does my library already do to support this goal? *Answer may be a service, program, partnership, policy, or facility-related task.*	What could my library be doing to support this goal? *Answer may be a service, program, partnership, policy, or facility-related idea.*
NO POVERTY		

	What does my library already do to support this goal? *Answer may be a service, program, partnership, policy, or facility-related task.*	What could my library be doing to support this goal? *Answer may be a service, program, partnership, policy, or facility-related idea.*
ZERO HUNGER		
GOOD HEALTH AND WELL-BEING		
QUALITY EDUCATION		
GENDER EQUALITY		
CLEAN WATER AND SANITATION		
AFFORDABLE AND CLEAN ENERGY		

	What does my library already do to support this goal? *Answer may be a service, program, partnership, policy, or facility-related task.*	What could my library be doing to support this goal? *Answer may be a service, program, partnership, policy, or facility-related idea.*
DECENT WORK AND ECONOMIC GROWTH		
INDUSTRY, INNOVATION, AND INFRASTRUCTURE		
REDUCED INEQUALITIES		
SUSTAINABLE CITIES AND COMMUNITIES		
RESPONSIBLE CONSUMPTION AND PRODUCTION		
CLIMATE ACTION		

	What does my library already do to support this goal? *Answer may be a service, program, partnership, policy, or facility-related task.*	What could my library be doing to support this goal? *Answer may be a service, program, partnership, policy, or facility-related idea.*
LIFE BELOW WATER		
LIFE ON LAND		
PEACE, JUSTICE, AND STRONG INSTITUTIONS		
PARTNERSHIPS FOR THE GOALS		

BEYOND SUSTAINABILITY

CONCEPTUALLY, IF SUSTAINABILITY REFERS TO OUR capacity to endure, this is a rather low level of existence. I doubt that simply "enduring" is our goal. To be sure, it is a first step. The first goal we have is to ensure that our people and our planet survive.

We also need to consider two other states of being: resilience and regeneration.

Shortly after we purchased our first home, we had an ice storm that bowed a stand of birch trees outside my kitchen window. I shared this observation with a coworker, a longtime gardener and homeowner, and asked for her advice. I was wondering if I should pull the trees back into position, perhaps create a structure to help them stand straight again. My coworker said no, that if I did that I'd weaken their ability to remain flexible, that they would, all on their own, rebound into their former position. I argued my position again, and she said that if I insisted on my intervention, I'd likely create a situation in which the trees would snap in half during subsequent ice storms because they would not "learn to flex and bounce back." Her advice paid off. Although it didn't happen overnight, the trees did slowly straighten up. After an ice storm the next year, the same thing happened. Those trees have built-in resiliency: they have evolved to bend and recover from the condition they find themselves in but, in average circumstances, not be destroyed by those conditions.

There is currently a wonderful surge of interest in building library buildings that are net zero energy (NZE) certified—those that produce, on-site, the energy they need to operate the facility, often from renewable sources such as solar power. These libraries will be "off the grid," able to sustain operations during short- and long-term power outages while creating no or low impact on their operating budgets.

The city of Hayward, California, is constructing Hayward's 21st Century Library and Heritage Plaza to be a net zero energy building. The plan relies on a combination of energy conservation and renewable energy sources to produce as much energy as the structure uses, as measured over the course of a year (www.haywardlibrary.org/post/92885994134/what-is -net-zero-energy). This library will join the Chrisney Branch Library in Indiana and another California library, the West Berkeley Public Library, as the first public libraries to be NZE certified.

In nature or facilities, resiliency may be built in. In organizations and communities, **we have to build it in ourselves**.

To employ Sustainable Thinking as we are discussing it in this book requires an eye toward resilience. To endure, we need to bounce back in the face of disruption. We need to build budgets, buildings, and a team that can weather the storm.

To contribute to resilient communities, we need to learn to listen, build an effective response network outside our libraries, and be nimble enough to respond in the face of the unexpected—a tall order made easier when increasing the resiliency of your community is part of your mission as a library.

Inherent in disruption is the often unexpected nature of it. Sometimes disruption happens overnight, like Uber and Lyft; sometimes you can see it a week in the making, like a hurricane; other times it is like a slow-motion train wreck that for most, seems inconceivable, like the white supremacist rally in Charlottesville, Virginia, *in 2017*. People can become paralyzed, frozen, unable to react in time to mitigate damage or adapt in a positive direction.

To be successful, we—as libraries and communities—need to employ a strategic mind-set that takes risk management to higher levels. We need to develop libraries that are deliberately designed to anticipate disruption and proactively position the library to be a resource in the aftermath of various types of disruption, whether they be environmental, social, or economic.

Understanding how a change, shift, or major disruption may impact how we conduct our business is critical.

Get your binoculars out, be a pessimist for a day or two, think through the various worst-case scenarios your community and library may face, and start designing a future for your library that is ready for just about anything. Use this chapter's worksheet, "Continuity Planning," to think through various disasters and disruptions that have impacted other libraries. You can't think of everything, but a little preparation can go a long way in the face of minor and major disruption.

CONTINUITY PLANNING

Preparing for the unexpected can feel overwhelming. Start by breaking your response down into categories of library internal operations (e.g., budget, policy, and facility) and external operations (e.g., outreach, programming, and partnerships).

A simple way to get started is to review your library's business continuity plan.

What procedures do you have in place if your library is flooded? If there is an extended power or Internet outage? What if you find yourself at ground zero of political and social unrest, as Ferguson or Baltimore did?

_____

_____

_____

_____

_____

Is a plan in place so that staff are ready to act? If not, what is the first step to making such readiness happen?

_____

_____

_____

_____

_____

_____

_____

_____

BEYOND RESILIENCY

A RISK MANAGEMENT MIND-SET, NECESSARY FOR CREAT-
ing resiliency in a system or organization, can keep you in a state of
paranoia. This outcome is, obviously, not ideal.

Let's take a look at the first two levels of sustainable thinking: we've
discussed sustainability (the capacity to endure) and resiliency (the capacity to bounce back after disruption). Both are necessary building blocks for
a solid community and library but both are tinged with a bit of despair.
One makes me feel like we're just keeping our head above water, the other
elicits a bunker mentality.

Our ultimate goal should be regeneration.

I first came across the term *regeneration* when studying for my Leadership in Energy and Environmental Design Accredited Professional (LEED
AP) exam. I was taking a course to become certified as a Sustainable
Building Advisor and learning about how a building works as an interconnected system within itself and the wider world.

I was fascinated by the idea that components of a building, working
together as a system, could regenerate or renew, and revitalize the environment. Again, I was struck by how this language translated to libraries.
Ultimately, isn't that what we're trying to do? To contribute to a thriving,
healthy society and civilization that can renew themselves?

Regenerative design is a systems theory–based approach to design. The term describes processes that restore, renew, or revitalize their own sources of energy and materials, creating sustainable systems that integrate the needs of society with the integrity of nature. The model can be applied to buildings, economics, and social systems. A regeneratively designed building might incorporate vertical farming on the exterior to cool the building and produce food, or it might generate more electricity than needed on-site to share with neighbors.

The revolutionary Living Building Challenge (LBC), the standard to build facilities that are regenerative, not just sustainable and resilient, has caught the attention of the library profession, thanks to an article featured on the cover of *Library Journal* in May 2017 titled "Net Positive | Library Design 2017." In the article, architect Jeffrey L. Davis of Architectural Nexus noted that though the notion of LBC may seem radical today, it was not too long ago that what has become an industry standard, Leadership in Energy and Environmental Design (LEED), was viewed in the same light when it first arrived on the scene.

The goal of regenerative design is to create systems that are so effective they enable us, as humans, to exist, thrive, and evolve alongside other species and nature at large.

Traci Engel Lesneski, a principal at MSR (Meyer, Scherer and Rockcastle Ltd.), an award-winning architecture and interior design firm, and frequent presenter at the American Library Association Annual Conference and the International Federation of Library Associations and Institutions (IFLA) conference, uses the term *generative* rather than *regenerative* as the ultimate goal in design: *"Our firm has decided to go with that term because it is more inspiring, and more broad. More about being net positive than about 'fixing' something, which the term* regenerative *could imply to some and which doesn't apply to every situation"* (personal communication).

That prefix *re-* implies that something needs to be redone or fixed, which may or may not be the case in a community. Things might be going well, and you want to add to that, to generate value across the triple bottom line.

The prefix *re-* can also indicate repetition. Looking back at its Latin origins, it was coupled with words meaning "again" or "again and again."

In addition to the well-established path of designing and operating facilities that speak to the concept of regeneration, the advent of makerspaces and hackathons at libraries often makes me think of a library's generative or regenerative role in the community.

When 3-D printers first came on the scene and the Fayetteville Free Library in New York kick-started the makerspace craze in libraries, many old-school library leaders were dismissive, thinking it was just the latest trend in technology that would fade out in a few years, certainly not something to redesign space and staffing patterns around.

But what the majority of the field was missing was the generative nature of makerspaces, the empowerment provided through tinker shops, repair cafés, and hackathons to those in our community seeking to make their world a better place. These services and programs, often brought to life with partnerships in the technology sector of our business and higher education communities, were not about technology but about teaching people *how to hack the world.*

In hacking parlance, there are black hat hackers and white hat hackers. Black hat hackers are those we fear, perpetrators of the coding mayhem that brings about criminal acts such as holding your data for ransom or releasing sensitive and personal information, invading your privacy.

White hat hackers use their coding prowess for good, to create solutions to societal problems through technology. For example, Urb.ag, a web app from Fathom Information Design, helps the residents of Boston figure out how to start an urban farm in that city. The app walks a potential farmer through the process of submitting applications, obtaining permits, and even attending public hearings if necessary, with all the information tailored to the exact code that applies to the would-be farm's address. This technology empowers residents with data to do something that is so basic—grow their own food, a particularly critical issue in urban environments.

When we think about teaching people to code, the conversation is usually centered on workforce development, but we should also be weaving in awareness of how to *hack the world for good* through this skill set.

Libraries that offer repair cafés are doing something quite similar. The extension of traditional library services to include not only lecture- or discussion-style programming but hands-on experiential learning opportunities empowers people to learn about the world around them and to take control of the multitude of "things" in their lives. An increasing number of items in our households—from our toasters to our computers—are designed to fail, designed to have an end of useful life to compel us to buy the next new thing. This built-in obsolescence is an economic, environmental, and, therefore, societal problem that adds to the toxicity and volume of our landfills and means more cash out of our pockets. Teaching people how things work and how to repair them can lead to innovative solutions to extend the useful life of an item or to re-create or invent the next new thing.

Part of being sustainable is lowering your level of consumption, part of being resilient is fixing your own stuff when it breaks, and part of being (re)generative can be inventing your own solution to meet your needs. These types of services in libraries speak to the pioneering spirit that we would hope to ingrain in our young people so that they have the skills to make the world better, on their own terms.

Nontechnical examples abound as well in libraries. From pop-up libraries to guerilla gardening to the classic town hall forum, many libraries are taking a page from the tactical urbanism playbook to create quick, often temporary, low-cost projects to make their corner of the world feel more lively or enjoyable:

- Oakland (California) Public Library: PARK(ing) Day, an annual event that takes over parking spots worldwide and turns them into public parks.
- Patterson (New York) Library: The Patterson Library Park behind the library facility includes an outdoor pavilion, lawn games, picnic tables, a community garden, and a tool lending shed.
- Rangeview Library District (Colorado): Anythink Block Parties—food, entertainment, and activities for all ages in neighborhoods throughout the library district's service area.

These are great examples of how libraries contribute to helping people not only endure and bounce back but create new and positive avenues to a brighter future. Use the "Libraries as Empowerment Engines" worksheet that follows to think through how your library helps people "hack the world."

LIBRARIES AS EMPOWERMENT ENGINES

How has your library provided a platform to inspire patrons to be innovative and create new solutions to problems they face?

_____

_____

_____

_____

_____

_____

_____

_____

_____

_____

_____

_____

_____

PART III

THE TACTICS

16

FROM THE INSIDE OUT

IN THIS BOOK, I AM MAKING THE CASE THAT IF WE FOCUS on thinking holistically and systemically about the sustainability of our local and global communities, we can help position libraries for the future in the strongest way possible (figure 16.1).

FIGURE 16.1 ——————————————————
SUSTAINABLE THINKING DIAGRAM

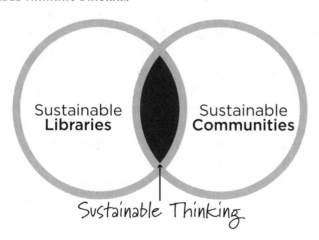

To do this we must adopt a core value of sustainability.

To make that work, we need to agree on the triple bottom line definition of sustainability.

To apply that definition in real life and achieve the widest possible impact, we must focus from the "inside out": from inside our library's core documents and operations to our external outreach for collective impact.

For a library to be seen as an authentic leader on the topic of sustainability, the application of sustainable thinking must start inside the organization.

We are very quick, as a profession, to jump to design thinking—designing programs and services for a perceived need.

No one area of library operations is unconnected to another, just as no component of an ecosystem is unconnected. So when we attempt to change course, we must consider the influence of our decisions on all aspects of our libraries.

You cannot force or superimpose a course correction or change; you must infuse an ideology. This ideology, once infused in organizational culture, is the guiding philosophy and principle that makes it all work. Sustainable thinking is all about thinking differently at our core so that every decision, every choice, every message speaks to that core. It is "systems thinking." When leaders and organizations think differently, think sustainably, their values and actions change accordingly.

Understanding first where we are headed and why is essential and is the reason that fully embracing the core values is imperative. If sustainability is a core value, then the Sustainable Thinking mind-set must be infused throughout our organizational dealings—from administrative and operational decisions to collection development, programming, and community connections. It is all "hitched to everything else."

Is a commitment to sustainability embedded in your library's mission statement? In its long-range plan? Has sustainability been adopted as a core value? Is it infused within library policy and management decisions?

If not, the other components of the system that make up your library organization will not thrive.

In an earlier chapter, we discussed whole systems thinking, a process of understanding how things and parts and systems behave, interact with their environments, and influence each other. This process helps us take a step back, look at the big picture—the biggest possible—identify root causes of a situation, and find new opportunities.

A "system" can be defined as a set of things—people, insects, your board of trustees—interconnected in such a way that they create their own pattern of behavior over time, coherently organized in a way that achieves a result. Systems "happen all at once." They are connected in many directions all at once.

> The system may be buffeted, constricted, triggered, or driven by outside forces. But the system's response to these forces is characteristic of itself, and that response is seldom simple in the real world.[1]

Owning the fact that what happens to our libraries is as much about our preparation and reaction as it is the outside force—whether that outside force be a hurricane or an e-book vendor—is critical to sustainable thinking for libraries.

Psychologically and politically we would much rather assume that the cause of a problem is "out there" rather than "in here." It is much easier to lay the blame on forces out of our control than to own the fact that our organization—whether it be on the governance or management side of things—was not resilient enough, adaptive enough, to successfully deal with a problem.

As you work to position your library for success in its future endeavors, you may focus on process or procedures, recruitment, and training. However, going back to the idea that systems "happen all at once," you will feel like Sisyphus, pushing the boulder up the hill only to have it come rolling back down time and time again unless you address the core issue—your organization's value set. The least obvious part of the system that is your library, its function or purpose, can be the most crucial factor in the system's behavior. A change in purpose changes a system profoundly, even if every element and interconnection remain the same.

So let's get existential. Why does your library exist?

Is it to circulate best sellers? Is it to build a birdhouse out of popsicle sticks at a summer reading program event?

Is it to engender a respect for lifelong learning, as so many of our mission statements proclaim?

Or is it all of these plus the countless other things we do and say that all add up to the idea that **we're here to make the world a better place?** And that the way to do that is by working toward liberty and happiness in people's lives?

I think most of us would agree. We are not educators for the sake of education—we are working toward something, we are helping bring to life a vision of a world that is a better place for us all.

The case needs to be made internally that sustainability-centric operations and outreach are key to achieving that goal.

In the next chapters, we will start the very specific work of how to deal with this sea change of a mind-set shift. You will learn about "change leadership," which will provide an overall framework for shifting conversations and activities in your organization to embrace sustainability as a core value. You will also receive a preview of some cutting-edge work that is being done by your peers to help libraries engage in very specific actions and activities for becoming sustainable.

NOTE

1. Donnella H. Meadows, *Thinking in Systems: A Primer,* ed. Diana Wright (White River Junction, VT: Chelsea Green River Publishing, 2008), p. 2.

CHANGE LEADERSHIP

CHRISTOPH LUENEBURGER AND DANIEL GOLEMAN, IN THEIR 2010 article for the *MIT Sloan Management Review* titled "The Change Leadership Sustainability Demands," outlined a three-phase approach for integrating a core value of sustainability into an organization.[1] This area is critical to consider given the scale of what we're talking about. To change the culture of an organization, you cannot superimpose or mandate; you must influence, partner, and lead the way forward, creating a tribe of followers who believe, as you do, that sustainability is a core value of the library.

Lueneburger and Goleman noted that your process should move your library from being

unconsciously reactive ➔ consciously reactive ➔ consciously proactive ➔ unconsciously proactive.

The authors posit that each phase requires different organizational capabilities and leadership competencies.

PHASE 1: MAKING THE CASE FOR CHANGE

Phase 1 is about building understanding and buy-in in your library. The sustainability leader needs to make a "clear and compelling case for change."

Take a moment to analyze your own understanding of the topic of sustainability. You may be the type of person who has followed sustainability issues for years and "lives green" personally. Or maybe you have sought out conference sessions that focus on sustainability, have joined the American Library Association's Sustainability Round Table, or have been saving up ideas for green-themed programming. At the very least you picked up this book to learn more about sustainability and libraries, which likely puts you ahead of most people in your organization. In all new endeavors in our libraries, we have to remember to bring people along with us to our current level of comprehension on the topic before we attempt to move forward. When people in your organization don't understand why you are pursuing something, it creates a lag between their comprehension and participation that slows down an effort or completely frustrates it.

Once you create a shared body of knowledge, it is easier to move forward as a team. This effort may mean education for your library's board of trustees, an in-service day for staff that raises awareness and understanding, or routine education for all library stakeholders about the very basics of sustainability and how it relates to your organization. In this phase, the library sustainability leader must be good at collaborating with and influencing others to create a shift in how people think about this topic. The goal is to help others transition from thinking of sustainability as a "go green" initiative with distinct boundaries (start and end; a specific service, program, or policy) to a holistic understanding of the importance of infusing sustainability throughout all we do. Using this chapter's worksheet, "Inch by Inch, Row by Row," you can think through who your allies are in the institution: Who currently has a similar level of understanding or a desire to help? Who has power and influence in your organization and would be helpful to do this work alongside? Once you have reached a new level of cognition on the topic as an organization, you can begin to have productive conversations about what it will look like for your organization to take a new world view in all it does—a pretty tall order. It's not like the new summer reading program theme or a new policy. We're talking about something that should influence **every aspect of library operations, programming, and messaging**. At the end of this phase, if done right, Lueneburger and Goleman predict that sustainability will "emerge as a powerful mandate that is pervasive throughout the organization."

In my own experience, once this phase is complete, others in the organization have taken strong ownership of the topic and have become sustainability leaders in their own right, an important guidepost to look for in order to judge when it is time to move on to the next phase.

PHASE 2: TRANSLATING VISION INTO ACTION

It is now time to use the momentum you have built within the library to effect change, real change, not just words about change but action. As the sustainability leader, you want to be results oriented in this phase, to get initiatives started that are clearly defined with measurable results. This is the phase in which you are moving the library from consciously reactive (this happened so now we'll do this) to consciously proactive (let's do this to get ahead of that) on sustainability "across the footprint" of the library, tracking economic, environmental, and social impacts over the planning cycle.

In this phase, successful sustainability leaders understand how to leverage sustainability into an advantage in the community. This may be where you partner with your municipality or utility company on a project or include the community in an energy consumption reduction or recycling challenge. Raising the visibility of the library through the conscious actions you are taking is an opportunity to tell the library's story, to show effort and impact, and to help model the way forward for others.

Leveraging your efforts to find community partners in this phase also positions the library as an expert in the community, revealing leadership potential in an area that other community leaders may not have previously thought of the library as participating in. This perception can lead to invitations, or "a seat at the table," for important community-wide conversations about resilience planning, risk assessment, and other types of sustainability initiatives. At the very least, your library will have a new level of awareness of these conversations in the community and should tune in when you hear of these types of conversations taking place. If you aren't invited, contact the convener of the event and get an invitation for the library. Just because organizers haven't thought of the library doesn't mean you shouldn't be there.

In this phase the library adopts policy, implements new procedures, tries a new program—obvious actions that commit the library to being a living laboratory in which stakeholders are empowered to find solutions that relate to the core value of sustainability. It is also in this phase that the sustainability leader steps back and decentralizes leadership, making room for others in the organization to take sustainability leadership roles in their areas of responsibility. When more people in the organization have a sense of ownership over sustainability efforts, new possibilities will come to light that never would have surfaced if the responsibility for "sustainability" rested in just one leader's hands. The collective wisdom of your library's stakeholders is an awesome thing—unleashing it at the right time is crucial in this endeavor.

PHASE 3: EXPANDING BOUNDARIES

In phase 3 the organization is continuously raising the bar on sustainability initiatives and leveraging sustainability to create competitive advantage. "A library seeking a competitive advantage?" you may think. You want your library to stand out in the community as a sustainability leader—how visible are you? Are you thought of as the go-to place to learn more about sustainability? Is your library building a shining example of how to create and operate a sustainable facility? Is yours the first organization that others in the community think of when they are looking for a strong partner to attempt a new initiative? Strive to be the most sustainable library in your county, region, state—the world!

As a sustainability leader, in this phase you need to focus on identifying and evaluating long-term sustainability trends, seeking new opportunities and working to position the library to benefit from them. The goal is to embed sustainability in the library's DNA—just as with financial accountability or intellectual freedom, the library should be unconsciously proactive about sustainability. "It's just the way we do things here" should be the answer when asked why you do something sustainably.

NOTE

1. Christoph Lueneburger and Daniel Goleman, "The Change Leadership Sustainability Demands," *MIT Sloan Management Review* 51, no. 4 (Summer 2010).

INCH BY INCH, ROW BY ROW

Who are your allies in your organization with whom you can begin this conversation?

_____

_____

_____

_____

_____

_____

_____

_____

_____

_____

_____

_____

_____

_____

_____

HOW WE GET THERE

The lack of resources is no longer an excuse not to act.
The idea that action should only be taken after all the answers and
the resources have been found is a sure recipe for paralysis.
—JAIME LERNER, ARCHITECT, URBANIST, FORMER MAYOR OF CURITIBA, BRAZIL

JUST START. **THAT'S WHAT YOUR BRAIN IS TELLING YOU.**
Just do something! Sometimes that is all it takes to make new inroads.

Or maybe you feel blocked or overwhelmed, which is making you feel paralyzed. You may think no one gets what you now understand. It's such a big concept, where would you even start?

Or maybe you've tried before and not gotten very far.

Wherever you are today, **there is a path forward.**

The key is to be methodical and to build your base of understanding and support to get good things off the ground—just as in any other successful endeavor you've been involved with. (Is this one *way* bigger? Yeah, it is. No one said it was going to be easy.)

Excuses are plenty—we don't have the support of our board or administration; our policy says no, we can't do that; or the perennial favorite, there's no money for that. All those excuses say one thing to me: the will isn't there. No one said it has to be done tomorrow, but I am saying now that action needs to start today. If that means taking a few steps back to get a better picture of the leverage points and the key decision makers and opinion leaders, well, then, do that work. That's your first step.

Wherever you are in your organization—from the office of the director to department head to frontline and operations staff—everyone can find a way to be a leader on this topic.

Mapping your organization to understand who the key decision makers and opinion leaders are is a great first step. Make sure you understand how things get done in your organization—for example, who makes policy? Who proposes policy? Who actually writes it? If you know where you're trying to go, the next step is to figure out how to get there.

Sustainable libraries need to get their own house in order if they want to build trust and credibility as a sustainability leader in their community.

You will need patience. **You will need to build support**. Tackling attitudes, procedures, and policy from the top down combined with grass-roots education and cheerleading will help all in the organization feel a part of what is going on and understand that what is changing is to help strengthen the library and its role as a trusted leader in the community.

Throughout my efforts to help libraries be more sustainable, as defined by the triple bottom line, I noticed that there was not a comprehensive way to help libraries work through this issue. Following my own advice, I approached the council of the New York Library Association (NYLA) to pass the first Resolution on the Importance of Sustainable Libraries in February 2014. With this buy-in from our professional association, we had a green light to pursue solutions to the issue. The council authorized the formation of the NYLA Sustainability Initiative Committee, a group I have had the honor of cochairing since November 2015 with my colleague Matthew Bollerman, director of the Hauppauge Public Library and a past president of NYLA.

The NYLA Resolution on the Importance of Sustainable Libraries "enthusiastically encourages activities by its membership—and itself—to be proactive in their application of sustainable thinking in the areas of their facilities, operations, policy, technology, programming and partnerships."

The charge of the Sustainability Initiative Committee (NYLA-SI) is to research and develop paths that would aid in bringing this resolved statement to life, to figure out what it would look like for a library to be proactive in its operations and outreach using a sustainable lens. The committee members agreed to use the triple bottom line definition of sustainability to guide their work.

Our twenty-five committee members are varied. They represent all types of libraries in New York State, predominantly public libraries but a few groundbreaking school, academic, and special libraries as well. Our committee represents all levels of work in libraries, from system directors and system consultants to library directors, frontline staff, staff, and trustee development experts.

Our committee members are called *co-creators*. What we are embarking on is new; we are breaking new ground, developing new tools, and tackling a very big task: to change the culture of libraries in our world. No small task, which makes sense because this is a very big issue. The co-creator model we've tried to develop acknowledges that no one person or leader has all the answers, that only by working together can we find the best solutions.

We have worked through multiple retreats to create four teams. Those teams meet regularly to tackle the work that needs to be done. The leaders from each team and the cochairs meet biweekly to check in and help one another. What has been created, in a relatively short amount of time, is a focused group of co-creators who are shaping the libraries of tomorrow.

Our teams include the following:

- *Marketing the Cause*—This team works to address a barrier we identified early on: people aren't clear about what *sustainability* means or what it looks like. Team members have created a glossary of terms, more than fifty "Sustainability Spotlights," online vignettes to illustrate what Sustainable Thinking looks like in libraries (of all types) in New York and beyond. They have produced an introductory video and now produce a monthly newsletter that has subscribers from all over the world to share even more spotlights, resources, ideas, and inspiration.
- *Road Map*—The Road Map team can take credit for producing the wildly popular *Road Map to Sustainability* booklet and mobile app (https://www.nyla.org/max/4DCGI/cms/review.html?Action = CMS _Document&DocID = 2068&MenuKey = SI). Another issue we identified at the inception of the group was the need to help educate library leaders about Sustainable Thinking and the triple bottom line. Education is key in this endeavor, and the Road Map resource helps learners capture their evolving thinking on the topic. It is a companion piece to the workshops and webinars that we do and serves as a Sustainable Thinking journal of sorts for leaders to capture thoughts at any conference they attend where an idea has been sparked or understanding has been achieved. Future plans for this team include

developing online learning modules to be used hand-in-hand with the Road Map.

- *Benchmarking*—This team has taken on the herculean task of creating a Sustainable Library Certification Program. The team has worked to create and assess a beta version of a custom process modeled on what has proven successful in other industries—from construction (e.g., Leadership in Energy and Environmental Design certification and Green Globes) to academia (e.g., the Association for the Advancement of Sustainability in Higher Education's Sustainability Tracking, Assessment, and Rating System and the U.S. Department of Education's Green Ribbon Schools program). You will learn more about this effort in detail in a later chapter.
- *Community Change Agents*—This team has taken a high-level approach to produce an experience-based learning opportunity for libraries willing to take the plunge into collaborative impact partnerships—a yearlong program in which a library and a community partner will have an immersive learning experience *together*. The result? We hope a team co-led by a library that effects positive change in its community by working collaboratively with a nonlibrary partner. We are excited to see what happens next!

We took the opening quotation for this chapter to heart: the lack of resources was no excuse not to act. We have done most of the work ourselves. We have received funding from our peers: the Leadership and Management and Public Libraries sections of the New York Library Association; the Public Library Systems Directors Organization of New York State; several public library and special and academic library cooperative systems; the Suffolk County Library Association; and two corporate sponsors—Sandpebble Project Management, whose owner and president, Victor Canseco, was an early inspiration and cheerleader for the work; and Capira Technologies, a New York–based company that *donated* its time to develop our Road Map to Sustainability mobile app for iOS and Android.

This groundswell of support is thanks to following the conceptual model in the preceding chapter. We started by making a "clear and compelling case for change." We're now working on translating vision into action, made much easier because we're clear on our compass setting. As famed anthropologist Margaret Mead said, "Never depend upon institutions or government to solve any problem. All social movements are founded by, guided by, motivated and seen through by the passion of individuals."[1]

The work of this band of professionals has inspired impressive action in a very short time. We have touched hundreds of librarians and library stakeholders through our efforts. We have inspired more than a dozen libraries to begin the journey to becoming certified as sustainable libraries. We are seeing boards pass new policy and make long-term facility and budget decisions based on what they are learning through our resources. We are changing the future of New York, together.

Excitingly we are seeing others follow suit: from ALA to the Vermont Library Association to the American Association of Law Libraries, other pods of professionals are unifying around the ideals laid out in NYLA's 2014 Resolution. This chapter's worksheet, "Be a Part of Something Bigger Than Yourself," asks you to do a little sleuth work. Does your state library association have a vision? If not, why don't you start that conversation the way we did in New York?

Our hope is that through testing our resources in New York and fine-tuning them, they will be even more impactful when they leave our borders. But for now, New York is clearly leading the way and, we hope, serving to inspire others in the library community to do the same.

We're all in this together.

NOTE

1. Margaret Mead, Wikiquote, attributed in Michael S. Matthews and Jaime A. Castellano, *Talent Development for English Language Learners: Identifying and Developing Potential* (Waco, TX: Prufrock Press, 2013), https://en.wikiquote.org/wiki/Margaret_Mead.

BE A PART OF SOMETHING BIGGER THAN YOURSELF

Check out your state library association's activities and resources on the topic of sustainability. Don't see any? Approach the leadership in your association about passing a similar Resolution on the Importance of Sustainable Libraries to inspire action in your state.

BENCHMARKS FOR SUSTAINABLE LIBRARIES

THE CO-CREATORS OF THE BENCHMARKING TEAM OF THE New York Library Association's Sustainability Initiative (NYLA-SI) have worked to identify benchmarks in the categories defined by the NYLA Resolution on the Importance of Sustainable Libraries (facilities, operations, policy, technology, programming, and partnerships) to answer the question we get quite frequently from libraries: *So how do we do this?*

It is clear that it is not enough to just understand the concepts of Sustainable Thinking and the triple bottom line; action is necessary, comprehensive action that makes a difference. Every time we do a workshop or webinar to make the case for Sustainable Thinking, there are inevitably questions about what practical steps to take next, where to start, and nervous questions about who would do the work.

We are not the first industry to methodically tackle this project. In fact, we are late to the game. As we looked around at what other industries were doing, we found copious examples of certification programs for buildings, organizations, and people. But as years of experience in libraries have taught me, librarians think libraries are special (mostly because they are).

Our guiding principle in this work is to help a library make balanced decisions that address all three components of the triple bottom line. Through such decisions the library will raise its stature among stakeholders as a community and sustainability leader.

Benchmarks are a standard or a point of reference against which things can be compared or assessed. Things are a whole lot easier when you know what you are shooting for. Much inertia in libraries concerning the topic of sustainability is likely related to feeling that people don't know what they don't know. They know about Earth Day. They know about recycling (sometimes). They know how to make a finding aid. They know how to make crafts with kids from upcycled materials. These things happen routinely, and because they are familiar and are forms of "low-hanging fruit," they can be implemented without overhauling the policy manual or holding a board retreat.

What we struggle with in our profession, in some cases though certainly not all, is the whole systems thinking approach to creating sustainable institutions that contribute to sustainable communities through the intersection of policy, staff development, building operations, financial planning, collection development, community involvement, and partnerships. This approach is overwhelming and mastered by only a few libraries that have visionary leaders and the right conditions on the ground to make holistic change possible.

The NYLA-SI conducted a scan of the various resources available to help libraries. The committee concluded that resources were already available to aid a library in determining more sustainable choices when it came to decisions that impact the environment, that we did not need to re-create the wheel. Use the worksheet "What Is Already Out There?" at the end of this chapter to do your own scan to find out what may be locally available to your library.

Early on in our research, we learned of a Green Business Certification process that the Hendrick Hudson Free Library (HHFL), located in Westchester County, New York, had undertaken. The results of this certification experience were so impressive that HHFL was awarded the Shubert Library Excellence Award by the New York State Regents Advisory Council on Libraries in 2016, arguably the top library honor in the state. The NYLA-SI is fortunate to count HHFL director Jill Davis among our co-creators. In fact, Jill took part in the very first co-creator retreat held in 2015. Jill shared her library's experience of becoming certified as a Green Business through the Westchester Business Council and helped us forge a relationship with the organization that created the Green Business Certification path that HHFL used.

We quickly realized that we didn't need to re-create the wheel on the environmental benchmarks and that we could expend our energies on creating custom library benchmarks to address the other two "legs of the stool." We have been able to negotiate a partnership with the organizations that sponsor the program that HHFL was certified under, the Westchester Green Business Council and Team Green Spirit, to allow statewide library access to their proprietary Green Business Certification program at a reduced rate.

However, this partnership left a number of categories and library-specific areas unaddressed—for instance, financial stability and sustainability; involvement with our community in a way that speaks to the Libraries Transforming Communities practices; and the behemoth in the room for libraries: our collections. To that end, the team undertook the development of custom benchmarks that help guide a library through policy making and decisions related to such categories as *Partnerships, Community Involvement, Social Equity and Resiliency, Financial Sustainability,* and *Collections* with the idea that these would make up the later sections of a full certification path for libraries through NYLA.

What we have created, and the council (the governing board of the New York Library Association) has endorsed, is a comprehensive certification path for a library that wants to step up and be recognized as a Sustainable Library. We have been bold and taken a run at defining what that looks like and pilot tested it. Is it perfect? Probably not. Is it a start? You bet.

In the next chapter, I've provided the outline of the certification path to help give you the scope of what is touched on through the process.

WHAT IS ALREADY OUT THERE?

Do a scan of your community, county, and state. Can you find a green business certification program that your library could be part of?

_____

_____

_____

_____

_____

_____

_____

_____

_____

_____

_____

_____

_____

SUSTAINABLE LIBRARY CERTIFICATION PROGRAM

THE NEW YORK LIBRARY ASSOCIATION (NYLA) IS PILOTING a Sustainable Library Certification Program to help public libraries work through the various aspects of embedding sustainability in their library and better position themselves as community leaders. The program seeks to provide a certification path for libraries just as the U.S. Green Building Council's Leadership in Energy and Environmental Design (LEED) program does for buildings.

To achieve the certification, libraries will engage in the following activities:

- Data collection and benchmarking so libraries can track their success as they progress through the program
- Policy writing to institutionalize best practices as a sustainable library
- Program and partnership development with an eye toward the sustainability of their community

All activities are designed to help libraries position themselves as sustainability leaders in their community.

There are twelve categories in all: seven environment-centric categories and five library-centric categories. All add up to helping libraries improve their triple bottom line as environmental stewards, economically feasible institutions, and institutions that place great stock in social equity.

The process kicks off with a *survey of library employees* to gauge staff behaviors and ideas about operating more sustainably at work. This exercise helps to raise awareness of sustainability issues and identify candidates for your library's "green team." The formation of the green team is another early activity of the program. A template of the survey is provided through the program.

Following is an outline and a description of the twelve categories.

Section A: Organizational Commitment

This section helps a library set the tone, from the top of the organization. There are fourteen related actions in this area, but the very first step is the passage of an environmental policy by the governing board to ensure that all are on board for the new sustainable mind-set of the organization.

Section B: Energy

This area has some of the greatest potential for making a difference, so it is pretty big! This section also has a policy component that sets the library on a path to prioritizing energy management. There are forty potential actions in this section related to energy audits, lighting, heating and cooling, appliances, and renewable energy. This section includes benchmarking energy use and conducting a greenhouse gas emissions inventory in the area of energy use so that libraries can measure success as they begin to make changes. Measurement is key to proving to internal stakeholders that changes are making a difference.

Section C: Materials Management—Waste and Recycling

Kicking things off with waste and recycling policy, this section touches on such issues as a waste audit, general reuse and recycling, paper and office supplies, kitchen issues, and your library's guidelines for meetings and small events.

Section D: Materials Management—Purchasing

Putting in place a green purchasing policy to define the parameters of purchasing more environmentally friendly products is the first benchmark in this category. Following that are activities related to centralized purchasing, office supplies, catering, green cleaning, electronics, and low VOC and nontoxic products. The section also empowers a library to take an inventory of current purchases and do an assessment of reducing consumption or switching to eco-friendly alternatives.

Section E: Transportation

You might not think about transportation from an operations perspective, but this section helps you think through employee commuting and business travel choices as well as how you might improve your fleet if you have delivery and outreach vehicles.

Section F: Land Use

For libraries that have grounds to maintain, this section helps you think through storm water management, irrigation, native plants, leaf and grass recycling, integrated pest management, and community supported agriculture.

Section G: Water

Water, water everywhere! This section helps a library conduct a water audit, think through whether the library's water fixtures are conserving water well enough, and address water-related issues in library kitchens, cleaning practices, and mechanical rooms.

As a capstone activity to this portion of the process, a library will complete a *Greenhouse Gas (GHG) Emissions Inventory*. Metrics include costs, use, and activity for energy, transportation (business travel, fleet, commuting), waste, water, and refrigerants. The data provide a baseline for current and future assessment and analysis of GHG emission reductions and controls as well as the framework for developing organizational policies and setting reduction targets along with specific strategies for achieving those targets.

Sections H through L are custom benchmarks for public libraries. These have been designed by the New York Library Association's Sustainability Initiative and were piloted in ten public libraries in New York of all shapes and sizes—from Queens Library, the busiest library in the country with multiple branches serving more than 2.3 million residents, to a small, upstate library district with a service population of just about five thousand residents.

The goal of these five sections is to continue the process of developing a culture in which these types of activities become the norm. Although libraries may be quick to check off things or groan when they see there is work to do, it is that work that will actually result in the necessary culture shift. *Sustainability is a journey, not a destination.*

Section H: Partnerships

This section helps a library participate in collective impact projects to help the library achieve maximum benefit for the community. Activities include partnerships with nonprofits and businesses, targeted programming, and innovative collaboration in the community.

Section I: Community Involvement

This section encourages libraries to get involved with community-wide strategic planning, staff participation in nonlibrary community events, and responsive programming based on community needs.

Section J: Social Equity and Resiliency

This is a large section encompassing a variety of topics that contribute to social equity and a sense of community to build the resiliency of the library and the community. There is a particular emphasis on promoting diversity, data-driven program decisions, and disaster recovery planning.

Section K: Financial Sustainability

A library's ability to pursue its mission is entwined with its financial sustainability. You should be planning to thrive, not just keep your head above water. Sustainable libraries are planning for the long haul and, therefore, need financial projections, fund balance development, and strong financial oversight of the funds invested in the library. This section also asks a library to think about recruitment and retention of quality staff and the long-term financial investment that is needed to pay competitive salaries and benefits.

Section L: Collections

Libraries devote enormous amounts of budgets, staff time, and square footage to collections, which means that human, financial, and environmental capital is expended for collection development. This section urges libraries to fine-tune collection development and weeding policies, use metrics to determine optimal collection size, and get innovative about collections and space used for collections.

Please note that sections A–G are proprietary, so we can't give away the specific questions and sample policies to libraries outside the program, but your state or county may have a similar environmental certification process—look for "green business certifications" or "green office challenge" programs in your area. Finding a geographically nearby program is really helpful so you can access the technical support and peer network that usually come hand-in-hand with these programs. That technical support is a big reason that NYLA-SI decided to go with the Green Business Certification program rather than create our own. Did we know the components? Sure. Do we, as library professionals, have the technical know-how to conduct GHG emissions, energy, waste, and water audits? Not yet!

If you can't find a local program, here are some leads to help you achieve many, if not more, of the same results:

- The U.S. Green Building Council's Leadership in Energy and Environmental Design (LEED) for Operations and Maintenance: Existing

Buildings Certification covers many of the same categories as the Sustainable Libraries Certification Program:
- Sustainable sites
- Water efficiency
- Energy and atmosphere
- Materials and resources
- Indoor environmental quality
- Innovation
- Regional priorities

• Green Seal's *Green Building Operations and Maintenance Manual* (www.greenseal.org/GreenBusiness/InstitutionalGreeningPrograms/ GreenBuildingOperationsMaintenance.aspx): Green Seal offers three versions of the manual, one each for the Northern, Southeast, and Southwest climate regions. The manual was originally written for use by public housing authorities, but the practices covered can be used for the operations and maintenance of a library as well. The manual covers the following categories:
- Cleaning Procedures and Products
- HVAC (specific to each climate region)
- Landscaping
- Lighting
- Parking Garage and Surface Lot Maintenance
- Purchasing
- Recycling and Special Waste Programs
- Roofing Maintenance
- Snow Removal and De-Icing
- Water Fixtures and Conservation
    • The manual also provides information on education, recycling programs, hazardous and electronic waste programs, landscape stewardship, community gardening, and composting programs. Swap out the verbiage of "resident" for "occupant," and the reading will go more smoothly!

- Check out the *B Corporation Certification Handbook* and pick out the items that work for a public library. The handbook provides interviews, tips, and best practices from more than one hundred B corporations. Although the program will not certify nonprofits, it has a number of attributes that you can learn from.
- School and academic librarians may want to check out the *Green Classroom Professional Certificate* through the Center for Green Schools at the U.S. Green Building Council. After completing the course and exam, participants will be able to do the following:
  - Support the health of school occupants, including teachers, students, and staff
  - Provide the best physical environment possible for student academic performance
  - Decrease absenteeism due to environmental factors
  - Support environmentally responsible practices by saving energy, saving water, and improving indoor environmental quality
  - Foster an appreciation among future generations for environmentally sustainable practices
  - Become part of the green schools and green building communities

TOP-LEVEL INFUSION

YOU MAY HAVE PICKED UP ON THE FACT THAT THE SUS-
tainable Library Certification Program is big on policy adoption. What we
have learned along the way is that the governing body of the library needs
to buy into, and authorize, the efforts surrounding Sustainable Thinking.

Key to this buy-in is education and public statements of a commitment
to support the work that needs to happen to advance the cause. Libraries
that skip this step will likely flounder and see their work fizzle out after
a year or two.

Organizational change is a large area of study. There are plenty of
change management books and courses out there to help you lead change,
from wherever you sit in the library.

However, I would like to share some thoughts on the importance of
focusing on the governing body of your library.

Public libraries are governed by the citizens they serve in the form
of a representative board of trustees or an elected municipal board that
oversees what amounts to the "library department."

When a public board is fulfilling its roles and responsibilities, it is
acting on behalf of its community with assets that belong to others—the
public and private donors who make public library service possible in the
community. Trustees are called *trustees* because they are entrusted with
resources that belong to someone else—the community. This profound

understanding, if extended throughout all decision-making, should naturally result in a board making sustainable decisions.

Trustees as well as library staff are **stewards of the public library**, and their choices have a large impact on the day-to-day operation of the library as well as on the long view of the library's future. Boards are usually charged with approving a long-range plan, an annual budget, and policies that guide the staff in carrying out the board's will on behalf of the community. These three top-level documents need to reflect a library's commitment to sustainability.

Just as the American Library Association has adopted the Resolution on the Importance of Sustainable Libraries, a local library board can adopt a resolution or pledge that states the board's commitment to creating a sustainable library and contributing to a sustainable community.

Libraries have a constant need to prove that we are a *good return on investment* to inspire our public and our taxpayers and donors to reinvest. Sustainable Thinking is an excellent way to expand community members' understanding that we are good stewards of their tax dollars, their education, and our local, and ultimately global, physical environment.

A community that believes in its library and views the library as a good steward of public dollars and the public's trust is one that will continue to support and invest in its library. This is the very cycle necessary to create a sustainable funding future for a public library (figure 21.1).

Acquiring sustainable funding for the library is one of the primary roles of a public library trustee. Implementing a strategy of Sustainable Thinking not just for library facilities and operations but for capacity building in the community is a long-term approach to stabilize, strengthen, and grow a library that can be responsive to community needs.

Responsiveness to community needs is at the core of our work as public library stakeholders. A library that does not reflect the values and priorities, hopes and dreams of its community is a library that will wither on the vine.

As trustees go about the business of governing the library, what guiding principles should always be present? In my experience, the compass point for boards has been to provide the highest quality library service possible with the resources in hand. Expansion of the available resources must be done with care and due diligence so as to not overburden the community, particularly in the area of taxation.

FIGURE 21.1

PLATFORM FOR SUSTAINABLE COMMUNITY INVESTMENT

In all things, a sustainable mind-set at the board table can aid trustees in making good choices for the community. The following are some examples:

- *Planning Committee:* A good strategic plan for a library is always rooted in community priorities, values, hopes, and dreams. A committee that takes the time to understand where it is in the planning cycle—whether it be on the eve of a new planning process or midway through an existing plan—should develop a system to routinely check in with the community to evaluate the library's reputation and progress. A *community-first* mentality in planning will have a ripple effect throughout the other committees' work. Board and staff members who understand why a community desires particular programming or why a community feels that a particular topic or service point is important can respond more efficiently in providing services and programming and promoting the library to the community.

- *Policy Committee:* Policies should reflect a commitment to providing a safe and healthy physical environment for library users and workers. This commitment could take the form of a purchasing policy that empowers staff to investigate products purchased for the library—whether we're talking about office products like paper, folders, and pens or about computers or furniture—that are produced responsibly and can be recycled at the end of their life cycle.
- *Budget Committee:* A sound budget takes into account cash flow, long-range plans, and economic stewardship. The director and budget committee are always looking for ways to accomplish what needs to be done within budget, to stretch dollars as far as possible without compromising service. The investment in sustainable strategies—such as an energy efficiency audit that will discover operational savings; the development of a sustainable fund or capital fund that can be used to invest in energy efficiency applications, say, for example, solar or building envelope improvement projects; or a continuing education fund that empowers staff to learn more about serving the community in a sustainable way—is thinking long-term about the library's viability. By thinking strategically, a budget committee can help strengthen the library for the long-term, not just "get by" each year.
- *Personnel Committee:* The personnel committee is charged with the governance of the library's most important assets, the staff. The people who deliver library services to our community make or break a successful library. Focusing on the health and well-being of staff, as well as on the retention of quality staff, is part of developing a sustainable library. Benchmarking salaries to ensure that all employed by the library are earning a living wage, investing in wellness programs for staff, identifying ways in which the library can improve working conditions for staff to instill a culture of care and respect for library workers—all convey to the library's workforce that the board understands and respects the value they bring to the institution. This care and respect are an investment in the future of the library, an attitude that should manifest itself through the staff and be delivered to the public in the form of quality library service.
- *Facilities or Building Committee:* This is the committee that you might assume would spend the most time thinking sustainably. This

committee, or a subcommittee, can focus on an existing building or be tasked with a renovation, an expansion, or a new construction endeavor. A committee of any category should receive education in the area they are tasked with making decisions in. Learning about the existing conditions of a facility, how a facility is used, challenges staff and patrons face in a facility is a good way to kick off a renewed sense of purpose for the committee. If dealing with operations and maintenance, the committee can ensure that it has benchmarked a building's performance so that improvements can be measured; commission an energy audit; develop a maintenance plan for the facility and major equipment to ensure optimal performance; and set standards for landscaping that take into account native plantings and water use reduction. If planning for expansion of some type, this committee has a much higher calling and, again, will need education about why sustainable choices in all things—from construction practices to low-VOC finish choices—are the way to go. A deeper understanding by the trustees tasked with working on the committee should lead to healthier choices, even in the face of slightly increased costs to do so.

In the accompanying worksheet, "Committee Charges," you are invited to work through the purpose and call to action for your own library's committees.

To empower a committee to work on those things that matter, as just described, there needs to be consensus about where we are going. This agreement will likely require a consensus document, such as a resolution, or the adoption of core values within an operating document, such as the library's mission and vision statement and long-range plan. The following are examples of such consensus documents:

- NYLA and ALA Resolutions on the Importance of Sustainable Libraries (see part IV, Resources, at the end of this book)
- The Presidents' Climate Leadership Commitments (http://second nature.org/)
- American Business Act on Climate Pledge (https://obamawhitehouse .archives.gov/the-press-office/2015/12/01/white-house-announces -additional-commitments-american-business-act)

- Kingston (New York) Library Climate Smart Pledge, modeled on the New York State Department of Environmental Conservation's Climate Smart Communities Pledge (www.dec.ny.gov/energy/53013.html)

COMMITTEE CHARGES

Review your library's committee structure—both board and staff committees. Does each have a written description of the work that members should be focused on and how that work will contribute to the library's overall mission and vision?

_____

_____

_____

_____

_____

_____

_____

_____

_____

_____

_____

SUSTAINABLE ORGANIZATIONAL CULTURE

ORGANIZATIONAL CULTURE IS A SYSTEM OF SHARED assumptions, values, and beliefs that governs how people behave in organizations. If our goal as a Sustainable Library is to take on the role of catalyst and convener to model the ideal and convene conversations that activate a community to come together in a higher state of understanding, respect, and empathy, we need to start by getting our own house in order.

Understanding. Respect. Empathy. These are fundamental building blocks of any relationship, whether personal or professional.

Within the Sustainable Library Certification Program, we promote diversity, a living wage, succession planning, and other human resources–related activities to help a library institutionalize understanding, respect, and empathy. But the truth is that you cannot legislate the human condition. Some managers will excel at promoting these values; others will have had years to cultivate bad habits that create destabilized relationships that promote division and distrust.

This process starts with you. Maybe you are a manager, maybe you are not. Maybe you are part of a union, maybe you are not. Maybe you are the director, maybe you are not. Regardless of who you are in the organization, you have a responsibility to uphold these values and help your coworkers do the same. You cannot control how others behave, but you can certainly set your own standard and control how you react to those around you in the workplace, just like you do at home.

So although we've spent a lot of time in this book talking about what kind of library you want to be a part of, please take some time to think about **what kind of leader you want to be in the story of the future of your library**. Everyone who works at the library is a leader, regardless of position or title.

Are you a source of inspiration for others? Do you work hard? Are you kind? Do you challenge the status quo respectfully? Are you energized by your patrons? By your community?

Are you willing to do the work to help make things better? Are you willing to work with others to make things better?

All these things are in your control.

As teams, we need to work to empower one another, to help one another's ideas come to life. My longtime coworker Merribeth Advocate (yes, that is her real last name!) always talks about the "wisdom of the collective mind." If we have agreed that to be more resilient communities we need to work together, doesn't the same hold true for libraries?

In the 2012 best seller *Antifragile: Things That Gain from Disorder,* author Nassim Nicholas Taleb pointed out that the resilient resists shocks and stays the same and that the "antifragile" is beyond resilience or robustness—the antifragile resists shocks and *gets better.*

This is what today's world calls for—that we do not hold the line for the status quo but that we seek to evolve and strengthen ourselves through the challenges we face as libraries and a society. Some of the best things about life today are born out of the good that comes from disruption. It may take a moment to realize that fact, particularly if you personally went through the disruption. **Our mind-set is key.**

We must create a culture of empowerment, cheering each other on as new ideas and ventures are created through collaboration and the collective mind—as long as we're all going in the same direction, why not? Hand in hand with this internal empowerment engine needs to be effective feedback loops and a culture of fast failure.

Examples of effective feedback loops are found throughout the professional library literature—team huddles, check-ins, staff meetings, 360 evaluations—whatever works for your library, great. But let's define *effective*—it is more than just updating one another about what we're working on. Feedback needs to be a thoughtful application of face-to-face meeting time that helps us advance on an issue. This approach requires that goals be clear, task assignments are made and respected, time lines are set, and accomplishments made along the way are celebrated.

Active listening, just as we've advocated for your library to do with your community, must also happen "at home," in the library. Communicating when there are obstacles, really listening when a staff person says she is stumped, are two parts of the equation that can become toxic very quickly when the intent is not for the sake of improvement of the situation but drifts into the category of venting or whining. Active listening requires that

> you make a conscious effort to hear not only the words that another person is saying but, more importantly, try to understand the complete message that is being sent.
>
> In order to do this you must pay attention to the other person very carefully.
>
> You cannot allow yourself to become distracted by whatever else may be going on around you, or by forming counter arguments that you'll make when the other person stops speaking. Nor can you allow yourself to get bored, and lose focus on what the other person is saying. All of these contribute to a lack of listening and understanding. (https://www.mindtools.com/CommSkll/ActiveListening.htm)

Another key aspect of the Sustainable Library workplace can be embracing the idea of "fail fast." Failing fast means that you quickly identify when something isn't working, learn from it, then rapidly move on to something better. Libraries are not known for this skill. In fact, in my experience, libraries might better be known for failing slow, if we'd like to coin a phrase.

Failing fast is not encouraging failure but **shortening the cycle time** of admitting something isn't working. Rather than drag out a program for multiple years that two people sign up for, let's close that down, assess what is behind the low attendance, repackage the program, and either try again or drop it and use the resources that had been going into it for something else.

We are not exactly flush with resources in libraries. Our frugal tendencies combined with respect of taxpayer dollars mean there is not a lot of fat in our budgets. The truth of the future is that what you are currently working on at your library is going to change. You are going to be asked to do new things. You are going to have to learn new things. You are going to have to talk to new people to get that new work done.

Inherent in trying new things is iteration. Iteration means trying again with a goal of getting to a better result. Think of software versions 1.0 and 2.0 or new editions of books. These are iterations of original works. They are not failures; they are **advancements, evolutions**. Software developers and authors are not self-defeated by having to try again; rather, failure is seen as an opportunity. Use this chapter's worksheet, "Failure: A Retrospective," to reflect on past failures at work and what you have learned from them.

If librarians could stop the self-flagellations long enough to shift their perspective when something is not going well, we will all, as a profession, be on a stronger course.

Every now and again we have the opportunity to hire new staff at the library. Are we hiring and training staff who can think on their feet, respond to change, and help the library and community bounce back after disruption? Thrive in the face of an uncertain future?

Staff development work provides a multitude of opportunities to strengthen our ability to be Sustainable Libraries. If you have the chance to influence staff development, I encourage you to think through these questions:

- How comfortable are staff with going out into the community, going where people already are, to connect with them about the idea and services of the library?
- Are youth services staff paying attention to education trends in your community? What would happen to traditional storytime at the library if Universal Pre-K comes to your school district? What will your library's response be if the school librarian is laid off at the high school?
- How comfortable are staff with technology? Can all frontline staff pick up the latest device and figure out the basics of it?
- Are staff monitoring trends outside the library industry to spot potential disruptions and opportunities in their local community?

- Are staff who are assigned roles of managing your online and social media presence conducting usability testing to understand how residents are interacting with your online presence? Do you actively work to increase engagement through social media? Do you have a responsively designed website that works on any screen (PC, tablet, or smartphone)?

Staff members who are empowered, engaged, and energized bring life to customer service, produce programming enthusiastically, represent the library in the community with passion and commitment.

When staff are empowered to make things better, to remove obstacles, to engage with the community through a new program or to be a part of something larger than the library—magical connections can be made that will serve both the community and the library.

FAILURE: A RETROSPECTIVE

Make a list of things you have failed at in the workplace.

_____

_____

_____

_____

_____

_____

What have you learned from these experiences?

_____

_____

_____

_____

_____

_____

23

INCREASING ECOLOGICAL INTELLIGENCE

Our world of material abundance comes with a hidden price tag. We cannot see the extent to which the things we buy and use daily have other kinds of costs—their toll on the planet, on consumer health, and on the people whose labor provides us our comforts and necessities. We go through our daily life awash in a sea of things we buy, use, and throw away, waste, or save. Each of those things has its own history and its own future, backstories . . . along the way from the initial extraction or concoction of its ingredients, during its manufacture and transport, through the subtle consequences of its use in our homes and workplaces, the day we dispose of it. And yet these unseen impacts of all that stuff may be their most important aspect.

—DANIEL GOLEMAN, *ECOLOGICAL INTELLIGENCE*

A LINCHPIN IN THE SUCCESS OR FAILURE OF A LIBRARY to be sustainable is ecological intelligence. All things are connected, and that interconnection starts in the natural world, which predates the human society and fiscal economy we have created.

Although I spend a lot of time explaining that no, sustainability is not just about going green, it *is* one-third of the equation. It *is* intricately intertwined with the other two-thirds of the triple bottom line. Some aspects can stand on their own; others are inextricably linked within one or both of the other legs of the stool.

It is critical that staff education be a component of your plan to become more sustainable. Every staff person is involved with something that is covered in the outline of the Sustainable Library Certification path.

For staff who work on maintaining and improving your facilities, providing education for them about why you might be advocating to change the way they do things or change the products they are using is essential. When people understand *"the why behind the what,"* they are much more apt to get on board. If at all possible, engage in an event with facility staff during which the challenges are laid out for them, indoor air quality issues are addressed, and longevity of systems is explained and then work with them to create a new way of doing things. Facilitating an opportunity for your staff to have ownership over improvements in your processes is another key to building buy-in for changing the way things are done.

Build in checkpoints to ensure that new ways of doing things are actually being done. A facilities manager for a local school district here in New York shared that the cleaning staff in one of the district's buildings felt that the new "green cleaning products" were not getting the school as clean as the old products did. As a result, cleaning staff members were purchasing harsher products on their own, with their own money, to clean bathrooms in the school. This was not insurrection for insurrection's sake; these staff members were genuinely concerned that the facility was not getting clean enough and that substandard cleanliness would jeopardize the children who attended their school. Educating the staff about the effectiveness of different products as well as the benefits to the indoor environment may need to be a part of the plan.

A variety of free green operations and maintenance (O&M) manuals are available online. Some are for housing authorities, others for schools, but search them out, and, if possible, find one that is specific to your region of the country. Regionalism is important! For example, if you live in the North, you will want to find a manual that discusses de-icing and snow removal.

Having a written plan helps codify a sustainable approach. A written plan can provide guidance, clarity, and specifications that help establish routines to improve the everyday, every year care of your facility. It becomes a training document and, essentially, a policy of the library, which aids in enforcement. One of the biggest struggles when getting people to think more sustainably is changing habits. It is often no more effort to do things in a new way; it is just remembering to do things in the new way and doing them consistently that is often the barrier.

Buildings are for humans, and a recognition of how people behave in and interact with the facility is just as important as the cleaning or landscaping plan. If the people using the building find ways around the operations and maintenance plans you put in place or do not have the same mind-set that created your plan, much good can be undone.

Staff who are charged with purchasing materials, goods, and services for library operations and programs are another group that will thrive with some education. At my organization, when we did just a small amount of education for our purchasing agent about what labels and terms to look for when purchasing products like office supplies, hospitality items, and cleaning products, we saw an immediate result. We were also able to bust the myth that going green would cost more because many of the products that were more responsibly produced and that we ended up switching to cost the same or even less than the previous products.

> Environmentally Preferable Purchasing (EPP) or Green Purchasing is generally defined as purchasing a product that has a lesser or reduced negative effect or increased positive effect on human health and the environment, when compared with competing products that serve the same purpose.[1]

If you are looking for talking points about why buying green matters, policy considerations when drafting an EPP policy, and tips for implementing strategies for EPP, the *NASPO Green Purchasing Guide* is a great place to start (www.naspo.org/green/index.html). The guide provides excellent advice for talking about the best value versus the lowest price, something public agencies must be very good at explaining when a taxpayer may judge a purchase on the price alone.

Determining the best product will likely require you to think through such facets of the item as durability, where it was produced, and performance. This practice is called *life cycle cost analysis,* something procurement staff should be very familiar with to help use taxpayer dollars wisely.

Daniel Goleman, author of *Ecological Intelligence,* provided three principles of "compassionate consumption":[2]

- Know impacts
- Favor improvements
- Share what you know

Where to start may seem overwhelming. Use this chapter's worksheet, "Start Small: Hospitality," to walk through just one small aspect of your library's operational choices. Practice thinking through each choice and what it says about your library. It is an easy entry point that may be simple to make improvements in.

Educate yourself—do not let the marketplace manipulate your choices. Learn about third-party certifications that help industries be transparent about their practices and their products. The following are common certifications that library staff can benefit from learning more about.

- *Green Seal:* Green Seal is an independent, nonprofit organization that uses scientific testing and rigorous criteria to identify sustainable products. This group certifies all types of products—from paint and lightbulbs to cleaning products and paper products.
- *Energy Star:* Energy Star is a government program that identifies energy-efficient products such as central air conditioning, furnaces, refrigerators, lighting, and electronics.
- *The Carpet and Rug Institute:* The Green Label Plus program of the Carpet and Rug Institute (CRI) certifies carpet, adhesives, and cushions to ensure low levels of emissions.
- *Forest Stewardship Council:* The Forest Stewardship Council (FSC) is a nonprofit, nongovernmental organization that promotes responsible management of forests on an international scale.
- *Cradle to Cradle Certified:* Cradle to Cradle Certified products include building materials, carpeting, packaging, cleaning products, furniture, and more.

There are a multitude of other certifications out there, but buyer beware—many are certifications by the manufacturer or an industry lobbyist group rather than an independent, third-party organization that does not derive a financial benefit from awarding the certification.

NOTES

1. National Association of State Procurement Officials, *NASPO Green Purchasing Guide,* www.naspo.org/green/index.html.
2. David Biello, "How to Live with Ecological Intelligence," *Scientific American,* April 27, 2009, https://www.scientificamerican.com/article/how-to-live-with-ecological-intelligence/.

START SMALL: HOSPITALITY

Most libraries provide some level of hospitality at library programs or events—food, drink, and the accompanying plates, cups, cutlery, and napkins required to serve them.

At your next event,

- Consider the origin and nutrition of the food and drinks provided. Are they from a local business? Are they healthy? Is there a minimum amount of packaging?
- Take a look at your plates, cups, and cutlery—are they reusable? Recyclable? Biodegradable? Compostable?

_____

_____

_____

_____

_____

_____

_____

_____

_____

_____

_____

CONSTRUCTION AND RENOVATION
ONCE-IN-A-LIFETIME OPPORTUNITIES

I WOULD BE REMISS IF I DID NOT SHINE A LIGHT ON THE massive opportunity presented by a library's renovation and construction projects. These projects are often once-in-a-lifetime opportunities to create a practical, inspiring statement on your institution's commitment to sustainability in all its forms. Embodying the ethic of Sustainable Thinking into these large, expensive, and impactful projects can be a proud legacy *for your community.*

Imagine, if you will, a facility in your community that is so smartly designed that it

- Costs less to run than conventionally built buildings
- Produces healthier indoor environments for occupants than the average building
- Generates energy and water on-site, lessening the burden on already strained natural resources
- Provides a connection to the outdoors and promotes interaction with outdoor spaces
- Harnesses the energy and light of the sun to heat, run, and light the building
- Showcases local expertise
- Can operate during extended power outages

- Can withstand severe weather events
- Can feed the community—mind, body, and soul
- Serves as a point of inspiration and education for future generations

Utopian? Maybe. But within our reach if we're smart about it.

Don't you wish that facility in your community was the library building? Make it so.

Many programs are available to help your design team create a facility that is sustainable, resilient, and regenerative (and I will talk more about those later in this chapter); however, you first have to make a commitment to a guiding philosophy of creating a sustainable facility and have the willpower to hold your architectural team to that philosophy.

Carol Sanford, author of *The Responsible Business* and *The Responsible Entrepreneur*, provides the conceptual model of Levels of Thought that can help you design a progression of activities (see the accompanying text box) that will ensure a commitment to sustainable design throughout your organization and design team when approaching a large construction project. The controlling idea is that unless your team has come to consensus on beliefs, philosophies, and principles, then conceptualization, strategies, and design decisions will not hold because they do not have a firm foundation. For example, say you start at the "design" level of this model, insisting that an architect apply sustainable design measures for your building, but your team has not agreed that an energy-efficient building is a guiding principle for the design. Then, when the inevitable cost engineering begins, if the price tag is a bit higher on the design because of higher equipment costs, your center will not hold because not all players in the project share the principle that your building must be self-sustaining.

If you can design a process that helps bring your teams to consensus that

- *Beliefs* = Core Values of Librarianship
- *Philosophies* = The Triple Bottom Line + The Three Es of Sustainable Libraries (Empower, Engage, Energize)
- *Principles* = Sustainable, Resilient, Regenerative

then, when you get to the phases of conceptualizing and designing your space, everyone will be working toward the same compass setting. This is part of an integrated design process, a proven strategy for sustainable

---

LEVELS OF THOUGHT

Beliefs—how we believe "things work"
Philosophies—our approach
Principles—guides to action

Concept
Strategies
Design (most projects start here)

Audit
Evaluate
Maintain

---

design to ensure construction of high-efficiency buildings that cost the same or less than conventional buildings.

Integrated Building Design (IBD), also known as Integrative Building Design or Integrated Project Delivery (IPD), is an idea that has become increasingly popular, so much so that the U.S. General Services Administration (GSA), "responsible for meeting the space requirements of federal agencies," now requires an integrative team approach on its projects.

The idea behind IBD is that all parties that will be involved in the construction project are part of the team at the beginning of the project. This approach differs from the more traditional route that brings players in at various stages in the process, players who will then not have the same understanding of or buy-in to the beliefs, philosophies, and guiding principles behind the project.

The American Institute of Architects' definition for this process states that by "harnessing the talents and insights of all participants," three goals are achieved:

- An increase in value to the owner
- Reduction of waste
- Maximized efficiency

IBD breaks down silos in the traditional building process and brings the experts to the table from the very beginning of the project to look at it from a "whole systems" perspective. A whole systems mind-set assumes that individual parts and roles are better understood in relation to others. Therefore, in IBD all the players involved are asked to work together rather than on their own, from the inception of the project. This approach can better engage everyone in the library's goals, and in one another's goals, which can ratchet up commitment to the project—to getting it done cost efficiently without compromising the library's vision—and spur earlier, more comprehensive problem-solving.

Although collaboration and integrated design can and do happen in the traditional building process, IBD establishes a framework that increases the likelihood that collaboration will happen. That collaboration is worth the effort: when project costs are in the millions, we can't leave optimization to chance, and though nothing is guaranteed by implementing IBD, it is an accepted practice that produces results.

To learn more about IBD, consult the following resources:

- *Design and Construction Delivery Process*, U.S. General Services Administration (https://www.gsa.gov/portal/content/100803)
- "Engage the Integrated Design Process," Whole Building Design Guide, National Institute of Building Sciences (www.wbdg.org/design-objectives/aesthetics/engage-integrated-design-process)
- Marian Keeler and Bill Burke, *Fundamentals of Integrated Design for Sustainable Building* (Wiley, 2009)
- 7group and Bill Read, *The Integrative Design Guide to Green Building* (Wiley, 2009)

Setting your sights on using a proven certification path (LEED, Green Globes, etc.) can ensure that the building you ultimately produce will deliver on the promises made in the design—for example, a building that is highly energy efficient, has good indoor air quality, and has an eye toward water conservation.

Undoubtedly you, or someone you work with, will balk at using a certification path because of perceptions that "it will cost more." First, it doesn't have to cost more if you do it right, using IBD and experienced design and construction professionals, and second, this is old thinking—it's not just about the money. Keep in mind the triple bottom line, not just the traditional bottom line.

> High-performance green buildings provide the *best value for the tax-payer and for the public* [italics added] through both life cycle cost benefits and positive effects on human health and performance.[1]

There are three major sustainable design certification programs that take the guesswork out of whether your building will perform as planned. Certification programs provide design standards and metrics that are more likely to ensure that you are provided with a high-performance building.

- *Leadership in Energy and Environmental Design (LEED),* a program overseen by the U.S. Green Building Council, is probably the most recognized and used sustainable design program in the world. There are 706 LEED certified libraries, twenty-two of which are LEED Platinum. The holistic program has versions for new construction, renovation, and operations and maintenance that provide guidance and a points system to help you address the multifaceted nature of buildings. Many municipalities—from towns and counties to states—are adopting codes that require LEED certification goals. Implementation of the program does come with a price tag but so does not using a program like this. It makes sense to have a better designed building than to allow an architect to sell you on being able to "build to LEED standards" without becoming certified. Certification means you are held to a standard and can measure the results—something you want your architect held accountable for.
- *Green Globes* is similar, in many ways, to LEED in that it provides a holistic look at a building's sustainability and it works on a points structure. Identified differences include fewer categories of design covered, more technical assistance, and lower cost to achieve. Green Globes has remained relatively simplistic while LEED has evolved and is incorporating some of the most current thinking about sustainable design. Green Globes does not have the same recognition factor or the same foothold in the market: LEED has more than thirty-five times the number of certified projects compared to Green Globes. However, GSA does allow federal buildings to use either LEED or

Green Globes, acknowledging that they both provide guidance that is better than no guidance.

- *Living Building Challenge (LBC)* from the International Living Future Institute is the future. While LEED and Green Globes are about sustainable design, LBC is about regenerative and generative design that is actually an ecosystem unto itself. Requirements of the certification include net-positive energy goals, meaning the building produces all the energy it needs on-site, and then some. Certification also includes a "Red List"–free environment, which requires the project to completely avoid materials that are made with chemicals that are known to be harmful to humans. Although the program may seem over the top today, keep in mind that's what people were saying about LEED ten years ago.

In addition to these three main holistic design programs, there are programs that focus on energy conservation and efficiency. There is growing interest in these rating systems because multiple municipalities and the U.S. Department of Energy have established the goal that new buildings be built to net-zero energy standards by 2030.

- Passive House (www.phius.org/home-page)
- Zero Energy Certification, International Living Future Institute / New Buildings Institute (https://living-future.org/net-zero/)
- Energy Star Certification (https://www.energystar.gov/buildings/about-us/energy-star-certification)

After our mission to help create more sustainable communities in which people understand, respect, and have empathy for one another, decisions about our facilities are the next largest area of impact we can have through Sustainable Thinking.

NOTE

1. Kevin Kampschroer, Chief Sustainability Officer, U.S. General Services Administration (GSA), and Director of the Office of Federal High-Performance Green Buildings, https://www.gsa.gov/node/78027.

25

CATALYST AND CONVENER

IF LIBRARIES ARE GOING TO TRULY BE THE EMPOWERMENT engines that our communities need us to be, libraries cannot be passive.

When I was a kid, I loved to play soccer. I wasn't necessarily good at it, but I enjoyed it. Partially because my dad agreed to coach my team. I adore my dad, and spending time with him at practice and games, and the car ride to and from practice and games, was special to me. He was very good at conveying the rules of the game, very serious about player development, and he went out of his way to recruit kids that other teams didn't want. Our team was a nice group of kids who had a good time thanks to my dad, but I can't say that we won much. However, I prided myself on understanding the rules and doing my job on the field, because that is what my father instilled in me.

One Saturday we were once again scheduled to play a team that had a player known to be the best player in the league. He was fast. He played hard. He kicked hard. He'd knock you down. We were intimidated. We'd consistently lost to this team time and time again. As we went through the first half of the game, I noticed that he had garnered such a reputation

---

Some material in this chapter first appeared in my article "Don't Let This Moment Pass You By | Sustainability," *Library Journal* (July 10, 2017), http://lj.libraryjournal.com/2017/07/opinion/sustainability/dont-let-this-moment-pass-you-by-sustainability/#_.

that when he went to kick the ball, often everyone backed off. From his teammates to mine, it was as if the seas parted, and we all watched as he would aim and execute a beautifully launched soccer ball right toward our goal.

I had had enough. I kept looking around wondering why no one did anything. And then I realized, belatedly, that *I could do something*. I was empowered, through the rules, to cross the midline and get involved. *I didn't have to wait for an invitation.* I didn't have to suffer the "inevitable" consequence. I was a player on the field, someone who was supposed to be an active participant. I was not doing my job and needed to stop waiting for someone else to do the work.

The next time I saw this kick about to happen (to the point that he had enough time to actually back up to have more momentum going into the kick!), I ran up and kicked the ball out of his way back to our striker, who took it upfield.

We didn't score, but I felt like the MVP because as I ran up to interfere with the play, I could hear my dad cheering. He was so excited that I had stepped in and made something happen in the face of what had become routine failure for our team. I looked over to see him jumping up and down and cheering for me, something I honestly had never seen him do (he is a rather quiet and reserved fellow) for me, or anyone, and I could not have been prouder.

When I started in the library field, I was an observer; I had not gone to library school yet. I didn't necessarily understand how everything worked. I had a great boss who invited me to a lot of meetings with our member libraries so I could learn. I thought of my role as that of an observer, diligently taking notes and learning from the expert practitioners in the room.

However, what I spotted was an unfortunate pattern. Far too often I sat in meetings in which library staff and administrators were straight-out whining about not being included:

"The teachers don't have time for us, they ignore us, they could care less about summer reading."

"The mayor held a meeting on education and didn't even invite us!"

"The county literacy volunteers got together and didn't tell us!"

I kept silently thinking, "So . . . do something about it."

The leaders in the library profession whom I am most impressed with make things happen. They knock on the door. Make the call. Introduce themselves. They ensure that they are in the right place at the right time. They ask to be invited. If no one is doing something, they get the ball rolling. They are catalysts.

When you understand what needs to happen, you have clarity of vision for the future, you know—just know—that your library needs to be a part of something or be on someone's radar—*MAKE IT HAPPEN*. Don't wait for someone to do it for you.

Mahatma Gandhi, the leader of the Indian independence movement against British rule and who employed nonviolent civil disobedience that sparked civil rights movements around the world, once said,

> We but mirror the world. All the tendencies present in the outer world are to be found in the world of our body. If we could change ourselves, the tendencies in the world would also change. As a man changes his own nature, so does the attitude of the world change towards him. This is the divine mystery supreme. A wonderful thing it is and the source of our happiness. We need not wait to see what others do.

Be the change, spark the change, lead the change. You will inspire others.

It starts with you, but the power lies in your institution participating, actively, sometimes in the lead.

Be a catalyst. Spark conversation in the community, speak with leaders in the community who believe, as you do, that things can be better, particularly if you work together.

Lead by example. Think everyone should be building green? Let's start at the library. Think everyone should pay a living wage? Start at the library.

Embrace the role of connector. Introduce people who should know each other to amplify their good work. Find the expert and give that person a platform at the library. Boldly introduce yourself to people you admire, to people who are leading the way, to people who are looking for a place to belong.

Convene conversations that make a difference. Think more energy should be put into encouraging small businesses? Convene a small-business summit. Concerned that multiple groups seem to be working on the same thing but not talking to each other? Host a meet-up at the library. The worksheet "Let's Get Started" at the end of this chapter is a framework to help you create your own action plan, from wherever you sit in the organization. We can all be leaders if we put our mind to it.

In 2017 I participated in an event cosponsored by the Queens Library and the New York Library Association entitled "Agents of Change: The Importance of Sustainability in Public Schools, Universities, and Libraries."

The event featured a who's who of sustainability leadership in the largest city in the United States—New York:

- Mark Chambers, director, Mayor's Office of Sustainability
- Meredith McDermott, director of sustainability, New York City Department of Education (the largest school system in the country)
- Tria Case, university director of sustainability and NYSolar Smart, The City University of New York
- Alex Mikszewski, energy manager, Brooklyn Public Library System
- Garrett Bergen, associate director of facilities management, New York Public Library
- Tameka Pierre-Louis, sustainability and energy liaison officer, Queens Library

The event, organized by Ms. Pierre-Louis, was designed to bring together education leaders who could have a big impact on OneNYC—New York City's blueprint for "inclusive climate action for all New Yorkers across four key visions of Growth, Equity, Sustainability, and Resiliency." This plan is directed toward the citywide commitment to reduce greenhouse gas emissions by 80 percent by 2050 with new investments in renewable energy, electric vehicles, and solid waste management to help improve air quality across the city and bring about an important shift away from carbon-intensive sources of energy.

Libraries were not just at the table for this event; libraries were the catalyst for the event—the event was convened by library people, held at the busiest library in the country, and cosponsored by the state library association.

Pierre-Louis did not wait for an invitation to the table—she made the damn table herself. She saw a need and did what library people need to do—she brought together the experts, the people who can make something happen, and made the introductions, the connections, that their city needs to be successful in their plan. She created a critical network for people to learn from one another, to cheer one another on and forged a new path forward to help one city's educators be the leaders their city needs in the face of the climate crisis.

Be the leader. Own the role. Inside your library and out in the community. This, more than anything, is what we need to build understanding, respect, and empathy among our neighbors and for our libraries.

Sustainable Thinking provides the conceptual framework for you to amplify the good your library will do in the world. It may mean talking about what you do in a different way. It may mean doing things differently. It certainly means taking responsibility for how your library is viewed and where you, as an individual, decide to expend your energy in your work.

Things are only going to get better if we work together. Libraries are perfectly positioned to be the heroes that our communities need right now, if we're brave and bold enough to step up.

NOTE

1. "From the Collected Works of M. K. Gandhi, vol. 13, chap. 153, 'General Knowledge about Health'" (p. 241), printed in Indian Opinion, September 8, 1913, Publications Division, New Delhi, India.

LET'S GET STARTED

What is your first step to helping your library be more sustainable?

_____

_____

Who will be your ally in making that first step successful?

_____

_____

What do others in your organization need to know and understand for your first step to be successful?

_____

_____

What is a reasonable amount of time for you to see signs of your success?

_____

_____

What are you waiting for?

_____

_____

PART IV

RESOURCES

AMERICAN LIBRARY ASSOCIATION'S RESOLUTION ON THE IMPORTANCE OF SUSTAINABLE LIBRARIES

Whereas our communities are faced with economic, environmental and societal changes that are of great concern to our quality of life;

Whereas libraries are uniquely positioned and essential to build the capacity of the communities they serve to become sustainable, resilient and regenerative;

Whereas library leaders, and those who inspire future library leaders, have a mandate to ensure future access to economical library services;

Whereas libraries that demonstrate good stewardship of the resources entrusted to them can build community support that leads to sustainable funding;

Whereas the people who work in our libraries and those who access services in our facilities deserve a healthy environment in which to do so;

Whereas the Intergovernmental Panel on Climate Change (IPCC) has determined that: "Human influence on the climate system is clear . . . Recent climate changes have had widespread impacts on human and natural systems";

Whereas the American Library Association has acknowledged in its 2015 Strategic Plan that "Libraries are widely recognized as key players in economic development, in building strong and vibrant communities, and in sustaining a strong democracy" and launched the ALA Center for Civic Life (CCL) in 2010 in conjunction with the Kettering Foundation to promote community engagement and foster public deliberation through libraries; and

Whereas libraries that demonstrate leadership in making sustainable decisions that positive address climate change, respect and use natural resources, and create healthy indoor and outdoor environments will stabilize and reduce their long-term energy costs, help build more sustainable communities, and thereby increase community support for the library; now, therefore, be it

Resolved, that the American Library Association (ALA), on behalf of its members:

1. recognizes the important and unique role libraries play in wider community conversations about resiliency, climate change, and a sustainable future and begins a new era of thinking sustainably in order to consider the economic, environmental and socially equitable viability of choices made on behalf of the association;

2. enthusiastically encourages activities by itself, its membership, library schools and state associations to be proactive in their application of sustainable thinking in the areas of facilities, operations, policy, technology, programming, partnerships and library school curricula; and

3. directs the ALA Executive Director to pursue sustainable choices when planning conferences and meetings and to actively promote best practices of sustainability through ALA publications, research and educational opportunities to reach our shared goal of vital, visible and viable libraries for the future.

Adopted by the Council of the American Library Association
Sunday, June 28, 2015, in San Francisco, California

NEW YORK LIBRARY ASSOCIATION'S RESOLUTION ON THE IMPORTANCE OF SUSTAINABLE LIBRARIES

Whereas, libraries are essential to the communities they serve; and

Whereas, library leaders have a mandate to ensure future access to economical library services; and

Whereas, libraries that demonstrate good stewardship of the resources entrusted to them can build their base of support in their communities which leads to sustainable funding; and

Whereas, the scientific community has clearly communicated that current trends in climate change are of great concern to all; and

Whereas, the people who work in our libraries and access services in our facilities deserve a healthy environment in which to do so; and

Whereas, libraries who demonstrate leadership in making sustainable decisions that help to positively address climate change, respect natural resources and create healthy indoor and outdoor environments will stabilize and reduce their long-term energy costs, increase the support for the library in their community; and reveal new sources of funding; therefore be it

Resolved, that the New York Library Association, on behalf of its members, recognizes the important role libraries can play in larger community conversations about resiliency, climate change, and a sustainable future; and be it further

Resolved, that the New York Library Association enthusiastically encourages activities by its membership—and itself—to be proactive in their application of sustainable thinking in the areas of their facilities, operations, policy, technology, programming and partnerships.

Drafted for consideration by Rebekkah Smith Aldrich, NYLA Councilor-at-Large-Coordinator for Library SustainabilityMid-Hudson Library System103 Market Street, Poughkeepsie, NY 12601
Adopted by NYLA Council, February 6, 2014

CASE STUDY:
KINGSTON (NEW YORK) LIBRARY
CLIMATE SMART PLEDGE

LIBRARY AS "LIVING LABORATORY"

Kingston Library in New York serves the twenty-four thousand residents of the city of Kingston. This is a library that "thinks globally and acts locally" and has taken deliberate steps toward becoming a green library. Members of the library's board of trustees have acknowledged their understanding that climate change poses a real and increasing threat to our local and global environments, endangering the world's infrastructure, economy, and livelihoods. To that end, they have pledged to make decisions that reduce greenhouse gas emissions and adapt to a changing climate through planning, library facility operations, library programs, and an evolving and adaptive process.

To begin its efforts, the library first decided to support the City of Kingston's Climate Smart Communities and Green Jobs Pledge,[1] adapting the pledge to work for a public library. The library's board of trustees passed a *Climate Smart Community Library Pledge*[2] in September 2010. This pledge states, unequivocally, the board's support of the city's goals to reduce greenhouse gas emissions, mitigate storm water management issues, and create green jobs; board members' comprehension of the impact of climate change on the wider world; and the board's intent, as the governing body of the city's public library, to take steps to be good stewards of public dollars and the local and global environments.

The library's efforts began in the right place—at the beginning—with the creation of the *Kingston Library Climate Smart Advisory Committee (CSAC)*, which was tasked with undertaking a benchmarking process to gather and track data on greenhouse gas emissions and to provide community programming to educate the public about climate change and related issues.

The library building is a former elementary school dating to 1878. The building's footprint occupies just fewer than eight thousand square feet and supports a total interior area of about twenty-four thousand square feet, including the basement. The site is a full city block and includes a parking lot of twenty-six thousand square feet. The library has occupied the two-story brick building since 1978 but has been fully responsible for its upkeep and improvement only since acquiring it from the school district in 2004. Natural gas is used for space heating and hot water.

Since the library became responsible for the facility, numerous energy efficiency efforts have been implemented—a *new roof covering, attic insulation, lighting upgrades, and window replacement.* The roof covering and attic insulation were part of a larger structural repair to the building roof. Some members of the CSAC were involved in these initial efforts for energy conservation and promoted the *analysis of energy use over time to validate the effectiveness of these improvements.*

The CSAC *gathered and analyzed utility data,* used an energy performance measuring tool, and authorized a new energy audit to aid benchmarking efforts. Committee members pursued a simple way to understand energy consumption by gathering utility bills (natural gas and electricity) and entering the data into a spreadsheet program.

To track and compare the library's performance over the years and to compare the library building with similar buildings around the United States, the committee used Portfolio Manager, an online tool created by the U.S. Environmental Protection Agency (EPA).[3] Portfolio Manager requires basic information about the building and grounds, including gross floor space (24,651 square feet), usable space (16,435 square feet), parking lot area, hours of operation (fifty-one hours per week), number of full-time staff (five), and number of computers (twenty-seven). Cost and use data from utility bills for natural gas, electricity, and water must be entered. The committee originally entered utility data for ten years (2001–2011) and subsequently added new data up to August 2014.

The EPA's Portfolio Manager is a free and fairly intuitive tool. According to the committee members, library staff members, trustees, volunteers, or consultants can teach themselves how to use the program, using training modules, FAQs, and other resources. The EPA's Portfolio Manager defines about eighty property types. Of those eighty, about twenty property types can receive an Energy Star Score, which compares similar properties nationwide, and can be eligible for Energy Star certification. At this time, libraries are not eligible for Energy Star rating and certification. Other benchmarking tools are available, both proprietary and free.

The committee took advantage of a *free energy audit* available through the New York State Energy Research and Development Authority (NYSERDA). This audit examined the building envelope and the systems for lighting, space heating and cooling, and water heating. It included an inventory of equipment. Data from one year of utility bills were used. The committee noted that although neither a blower door test nor an infrared examination of the building was done during this audit, the audit nevertheless provided the committee with important information about how the library was using energy and, therefore, how to reduce energy use.

As mentioned, the audit indicated *how the library was using energy*. Space heating used the most energy and, therefore, cost the most. Lighting and air conditioning were the next two most costly uses of energy:

- Lighting (44 percent)
- Air conditioning (39 percent)
- Equipment (17 percent)

Through this analysis the committee learned that two refrigerators in the building, used to house staff lunches and occasional refreshments for public programs, were consuming almost as much energy as the computers and monitors.

The committee *learned from the audit* that the library should pursue further energy efficiency improvements such as lighting changes, weather stripping on doors, and occupancy sensors in the restrooms.

Behavior change applies to staff and patrons alike and includes such things as turning off lights and monitors, closing doors, and not using the elevator. Other behavior changes include recycling, reducing waste, and using alternative ways to get to the library (taking a bus, walking, biking, ridesharing).

The results of these efforts demonstrated that energy use per area and greenhouse gas emissions have been decreasing over time; that the library is performing well above average (the building is performing about 68 percent better than the national mean for similar buildings); and *that few improvements were recommended in the audit.* These results caused the committee to conclude that the improvements made in the past decade have made a difference.

Going "green" is not just about energy efficiency; it is about taking a look, holistically, at the impact that library operations have on the natural world. The library also pursued a project to manage storm water. As part of repaving the twenty-six-thousand-square-foot parking lot, green infrastructure was installed to handle the storm water flowing from the roof and the parking lot on-site and overflow handled by the municipal storm water sewer. This effort included disconnection of roof leaders that flowed to the sanitary sewer system and installation of a rain garden and dry wells. The system led to the reduction of four hundred thousand gallons per year of rainwater entering the sanitary sewer system; no rainwater from the library roof now enters the sanitary sewer system (www.dec.ny.gov/lands/86684.html).

The committee is currently *learning more about sustainable building operations to follow best management practices for waste management, purchasing, and building and grounds maintenance.*

The library recognizes that *it is part of fulfilling the goal* set by the City of Kingston in its Climate Action Plan to reduce energy use and GHG emissions by 20 percent by 2020, or "20 by 20."[4] The City of Kingston was recognized in April 2014 with a bronze Climate Smart Communities certification. The library also contributes to the New York State goal, set in 2009 by Governor Paterson through Executive Order 24, which established a goal to reduce greenhouse gas emissions by 80 percent from 1990 levels by the year 2050 ("80 by 50").[5]

The committee works in partnership with the city's climate committee and other sustainability initiatives. Committee members state that they are committed to engaging community members in meaningful conversation about energy reduction and sustainability.

CSAC chair Emilie Hauser offers the following lessons learned:

- Use local experts. The energy improvements, benchmarking, and communications have been helped by the voluntary efforts of sustainability professionals.
- Capitalize on the passions of trustees and other volunteers and their willingness to learn.
- Spend the time to locate data and enter them into a spreadsheet and energy management tools.
- Start with simple, low-cost actions. Not all institutions have the ability to pursue bonds for capital funds, but by using energy audits and other tools, libraries can develop plans to implement low-cost measures and raise funds for more expensive measures, saving money for the future and increasing comfort for occupants.
- Use energy audits and other services.
- Take weather into account. Find someone to help with comparing energy use to heating and cooling degree days.
- Form a support group of like-minded institutions.
- Engage the community in carrying out the process and in celebrating success.

- Recognize that energy improvements may be invisible to patrons.
- Remember that *"a decision not to install more efficient energy equipment and implement related energy-saving measures is a decision to continue paying higher utility bills."*

NOTES

1. The New York State Climate Smart Communities Program helps municipalities take action on climate change. The program is designed for municipalities, but libraries can benefit from many of the resources on its website.
2. Climate Smart Community Library Pledge, www.kingstonlibrary.org/pdf/trustee/kl _climate_smart_pledge.pdf.
3. The EPA's Portfolio Manager is an interactive energy management tool that allows building owners and operators to track and assess energy and water consumption in a secure online environment. This web-based tool is provided for free by Energy Star, a joint program of the U.S. Environmental Protection Agency and the U.S. Department of Energy (www.energystar.gov/index.cfm?c = evaluate_performance.bus_portfoliomanager).
4. City of Kingston (New York), City of Kingston Climate Action Plan (2012) and 2010 Community-Wide and Local Government Operations Energy and Greenhouse Gas Emissions Inventory, https://www.kingston-ny.gov/filestorage/8463/10953/10960/ Kingston_Climate_Action_Plan_FINAL.pdf.
5. New York State Department of Environmental Conservation, "Executive Order No. 24 (2009): Establishing a Goal to Reduce Greenhouse Gas Emissions Eighty Percent by the Year 2050 and Preparing a Climate Action Plan," www.dec.ny.gov/energy/71394.html.

CLIMATE SMART COMMUNITY
LIBRARY PLEDGE

SEPTEMBER 16, 2010

WHEREAS, the City of Kingston passed a Climate Smart, Green Jobs Pledge on October 6, 2009, and Kingston Library would like to show support for that Pledge; and

WHEREAS, the Board of Trustees of the Kingston Library understands that climate change poses a real and increasing threat to our local and global environments which is primarily due to the burning of fossil fuels; and

WHEREAS, the effects of climate change will endanger the world's infrastructure, economy, and livelihoods; harm farms, orchards, and ecological communities, including native fish and wildlife populations; spread invasive species and exotic diseases; reduce drinking water supplies and recreational opportunities; and pose health threats to our community's citizens; and

WHEREAS, we believe that our local response to climate change provides us with an unprecedented opportunity to save money, and to contribute to livable, energy-independent, and secure communities, and vibrant innovation economies; and

WHEREAS, we believe the scale of greenhouse gas (GHG) emissions reductions required for climate stabilization will require sustained and substantial efforts; and

WHEREAS, we believe that even if emissions were dramatically reduced today, communities would still be required to adapt to the effects of climate change for decades to come; and

WHEREAS, we understand that public libraries are good stewards of public dollars and therefore should investigate and invest in energy efficient cost saving options,

IT IS HEREBY RESOLVED that Kingston Library, in order to reduce greenhouse gas emissions and adapt to a changing climate, will take certain steps [outlined as follows]:

1. Planning

- Set goals to reduce greenhouse gas (GHG) emissions and adapt to predicted climatic changes.
- Encourage stakeholder and public input by establishing an advisory committee to review the issues and propose a plan of action including facility operations and library programming. Recognize that climate mitigation and adaptation requires behavior change and actions by the Board, Director, staff, and library patrons.
- Designate a joint staff-Board sub-committee who will oversee climate change initiatives and publicly report on progress.
- Work cooperatively with national, state, and local initiatives, including the City of Kingston's Climate Smart Communities and Green Jobs Pledge, to ensure that efforts complement and reinforce one another.
- Integrate climate change considerations into library activities, policies, and long term planning. Inform and inspire the public.

2. Library Facility Operations

- Gather data through an inventory of GHG gas emissions from electricity and natural gas usage, waste production, water use, and other sources to establish baselines for Library operations. Set up a procedure to regularly collect data.
- Develop quantifiable interim GHG emission targets consistent with emission reduction goals such as Renewable Energy Task Force Plan (2008) goal of reducing electricity use by 15 percent from projected levels no later than 2015; NYS Governor's Executive Order 24, which creates a NYS goal to reduce NYS GHG emissions by 80 percent of 1990 levels by 2050; and NYS Governor's "45 by 15" initiative, which requires New York to meet 45 percent of its electricity needs through renewable energy and improved building energy efficiencies by 2015.
- Develop an emission reduction plan that details how to achieve the targets, and includes a schedule. The plan should address:
  - Energy conservation and efficiency retrofits
  - Renewable energy

— Solid waste source reduction, reuse, recycling, and other smart solid waste management practices
— Water conservation
— Actions that affect or influence the community
— Purchasing policies for procuring climate smart goods and services
- Carry out plans to reduce emissions, evaluate progress, and make changes as required.

3. Library Programs

- Integrate climate change actions into library programs to inspire and engage patrons and the community.
- Provide opportunities to support community climate change mitigation and adaptation actions and a green innovative economy by providing climate-change related library materials, programming, and other resources that will help community businesses and residents learn about climate protection, sustainability, and environmental goods and services.
- Lead by example, by highlighting the Library's commitment to reducing energy use, saving tax dollars, and adapting to changing conditions. Report GHG emissions and targets to Library patrons and constituents.
- Demonstrate the benefits of recycling, water conservation, stormwater management, energy savings, energy efficiency, and renewable energy projects by regularly communicating goals and progress to patrons and stakeholders.
- Provide opportunities for the community to reduce their carbon footprint such as encouraging walking, bicycling, carpooling, and public transit for employees and patrons or by discouraging vehicle idling in the parking lot.
- Compare successes, cooperate and collaborate with community and neighboring libraries' efforts to redirect less-effective actions and amplify positive results.

4. Adaptation to Unavoidable Climate Change

- Consider the risks and the Library's vulnerability to unavoidable climate change and factor them into long-term decision-making. Climate change impacts that could affect the Library include increased stormwater and flooding, drought, and extreme and prolonged summer temperatures.
- Use guidance and recommendations from NYS Climate Action Plan and other resources.

5. An Evolving and Adaptive Process

- Acknowledge that research and policy on climate protection are constantly improving and evolving.
- Be willing to consider new ideas and commit to update plans and policies as needed.
- Monitor and evaluate progress and make changes as warranted.

AMERICAN COLLEGE
AND UNIVERSITY PRESIDENTS'
CLIMATE COMMITMENT

We, the undersigned presidents and chancellors of colleges and universities, are deeply concerned about the unprecedented scale and speed of global warming and its potential for large-scale, adverse health, social, economic and ecological effects. We recognize the scientific consensus that global warming is real and is largely being caused by humans. We further recognize the need to reduce the global emission of greenhouse gases by 80 percent by mid-century at the latest, in order to avert the worst impacts of global warming and to reestablish the more stable climatic conditions that have made human progress over the last 10,000 years possible.

While we understand that there might be short-term challenges associated with this effort, we believe that there will be great short-, medium-, and long-term economic, health, social, and environmental benefits, including achieving energy independence for the U.S. as quickly as possible.

We believe colleges and universities must exercise leadership in their communities and throughout society by modeling ways to minimize global warming emissions, and by providing the knowledge and the educated graduates to achieve climate neutrality. Campuses that address the climate challenge by reducing global warming emissions and by integrating sustainability into their curriculum will better serve their students and meet their social mandate to help create a thriving, ethical, and civil society. These colleges and universities will be providing students with the knowledge and skills needed to address the critical, systemic challenges faced by the world in this new century and enable them to benefit from the economic opportunities that will arise as a result of solutions they develop.

We further believe that colleges and universities that exert leadership in addressing climate change will stabilize and reduce their long-term energy costs, attract excellent students and faculty, attract new sources of funding, and increase the support of alumni and local communities. Accordingly, we commit our institutions to taking the following steps in pursuit of climate neutrality.

1. **Initiate the development of a comprehensive plan to achieve climate neutrality as soon as possible.**
   a. Within two months of signing this document, create institutional structures to guide the development and implementation of the plan.
   b. Within one year of signing this document, complete a comprehensive inventory of all greenhouse gas emissions (including emissions from electricity, heating, commuting, and air travel) and update the inventory every other year thereafter.
   c. Within two years of signing this document, develop an institutional action plan for becoming climate neutral, which will include:
      i. A target date for achieving climate neutrality as soon as possible.
      ii. Interim targets for goals and actions that will lead to climate neutrality.
      iii. Actions to make climate neutrality and sustainability a part of the curriculum and other educational experience for all students.
      iv. Actions to expand research or other efforts necessary to achieve climate neutrality.
      v. Mechanisms for tracking progress on goals and actions.

2. **Initiate two or more of the following tangible actions to reduce greenhouse gases while the more comprehensive plan is being developed.**
   a. Establish a policy that all new campus construction will be built to at least the U.S. Green Building Council's LEED Silver standard or equivalent.
   b. Adopt an energy-efficient appliance purchasing policy requiring purchase of ENERGY STAR certified products in all areas for which such ratings exist.
   c. Establish a policy of offsetting all greenhouse gas emissions generated by air travel paid for by our institution.
   d. Encourage use of and provide access to public transportation for all faculty, staff, students, and visitors at our institution.

e. Within one year of signing this document, begin purchasing or producing at least 15 percent of our institution's electricity consumption from renewable sources.

f. Establish a policy or a committee that supports climate and sustainability shareholder proposals at companies where our institution's endowment is invested.

g. Participate in the Waste Minimization component of the national RecycleMania competition, and adopt three or more associated measures to reduce waste.

3. **Make the action plan, inventory, and periodic progress reports publicly available by submitting them to the ACUPCC Reporting System for posting and dissemination.**

In recognition of the need to build support for this effort among college and university administrations across America, we will encourage other presidents to join this effort and become signatories to this commitment.
Signed,

———————————

The Signatories of the American College and University Presidents' Climate Commitment
(www.presidentsclimatecommitment.org/about/commitment)

LONG-RANGE PLAN EXAMPLE—WEST VANCOUVER (BRITISH COLUMBIA) MEMORIAL LIBRARY

"OUR VALUES"

Intellectual Freedom

We uphold free and equal access to ideas and information. We champion literacy in all its forms.

Excellence

We are dedicated to knowledgeable, friendly and helpful service. We pursue thoughtful innovation, respecting our valued traditions.

Inclusiveness

We respect one another and promote a culture of inclusion.

Integrity

We are dedicated to honesty and openness in all we do. We are accountable to the community.

Sustainability

We manage our resources responsibly to enhance our financial stability, social goodwill, and environmental leadership.

See https://westvanlibrary.ca/sites/default/files/uploads/board/2011_2015_Strategic_Plan.pdf.

INDEX